MAKING
THE
MESSAGE
CLEAR

HOW TO MASTER THE BUSINESS COMMUNICATION TOOLS THAT DIRECT PRODUCTIVITY, EXCELLENCE AND POWER

JAMES EICHER
FOREWORD BY JOHN GRINDER, PH.D.

Grinder, DeLozier & Associates

Published by
Grinder, Delozier & Associates
P.O. Box 67359
Scotts Valley, CA 95067-7359

Master Distributor
Metamorphous Advanced Product Services
P.O. Box 10616
Portland, OR 97210-0616

Copyright © 1993 by James Eicher
Editorial and Art Direction by Lori Stephens
Printed in the United States of America

Eicher, James, 1954 -
    Making the message clear : how to master the business
communication tools that direct productivity, excellence and power /
James Eicher
    p.   cm.
    Includes bibliographical references.
    ISBN 1-55552-048-0 : $11.95
1. Communication in management. 2. Interpersonal communication.
I. Title.
HD30.3.E36   1993
658.4'5--dc20   93-25973

Table of Contents

To my parents, Bill and Eva
with love and appreciation

Acknowledgments

There have been many people who have contributed to the making of this book—students, friends, acquaintances and family. However, there are several whom I would like to single out. Their help, assistance, and encouragement is very much appreciated and I doubt I could have done as good or as timely a job if it had not been for them. For their fine secretarial work, I'd like to thank Merilee Neggie, Pam Miura, and Sandra Malik; for their overall support and editorial suggestions, I'd like to thank Michael Suggs, Jack Dwyer, David Josselyn, Steve and Connirae Andreas, Mary Kay Lopez, Norm Matsubara, Jo Marie Ruckh, David Miklowitz, Winton Churchill, Dr. Paul Hersey, Judith Grinder, Dr. Robert Lorber, Judith Hubner, and Steve Weininger.

I'd particularly like to thank Richard Bandler and John Grinder, the co-developers of Neurolinguistic Programming (NLP) without whom this book would not have been possible. I especially thank John Grinder for his editorial guidance and support, and his warm friendship throughout the years.

A Note On The Paperback Edition:
The author wishes to thank Michael Moreau, Lori Stephens, David Balding, and John Grinder for their help and support with the paperback edition. Many, many thanks!

How The Book Is Structured

Each chapter contains from one to three key concepts which are discussed throughout. In general, the material in one chapter builds on the material which preceded it with each chapter becoming a bit more complex. The key concepts follow the headlines in bold type, e.g., **Preferred Sensory Modality.** Related concepts are in smaller type.

Each chapter also contains: sample case studies that serve as examples of the key concepts; idiomatic expressions which further serve to illustrate the key concepts and make them relevant to your business situation; a chapter summary; and finally a chapter action plan for further self-instruction.

To get the most out of the book, do the exercises in the chapters and follow the action plans at the end of each chapter. Both are designed to maximize your learning.

Foreword

It is a particular pleasure to write this foreword for James Eicher. Mr. Eicher has successfully interpreted the general patterns of communication excellence in the context of business—a task attempted by many but accomplished by few. Not content with a fine interpretation of these patterns of communication excellence, James Eicher has himself developed procedures, formats, and specific methods for improving business practice. His work addresses the core business issue—the relationship between productivity and communication. Altogether too frequently in the daily scramble to meet deadlines, in the ubiquitous meetings, in the high pressure of corporate decision making, good communication practice is perceived as a peripheral issues—a secondary consideration, even a frill to be disposed with if time constraints are primary. Eicher argues convincingly that increased efficiency and productivity are solidly linked to good communication practice—that, contrary to widespread opinion, the greater the time constraints, the more critical the communication practice. His exposition is simple, not easy but simple. Examples and step-by-step exercises deliver to the reader the central issues of good communication practice developed in a clear and enjoyable style in the main text.

On a more personal note, I am genuinely pleased with James Eicher's work. Some dozen years ago, a former partner of mine and I found ourselves in possession of a set of communication tools which had a revolutionary impact when applied to human behavior. To ensure that these tools were transferable in a cost and time effective manner, we selected a half dozen very bright young college students who had no background academically or professionally in communication. These were our "whiz kids."

Here is one whiz kid who grew up and to my delight, has

made good on that early promise. After a decade of experience in the world of business, he has created a balanced, perfectly understandable, perhaps most importantly, eminently usable model of excellence in business communication. My sincere compliments!

John Grinder
Bonny Doon, California
Winter, 1986-87

Preface

The communication models and exercises presented in *Making The Message Clear* are based on developments made in the behavioral and cognitive sciences over the past several decades. In particular, the models and exercises in this book are based on a theory of communication and change developed by John Grinder, Richard Bandler, and their colleagues termed Neurolinguistic Programming (NLP). NLP has found broad applications in the areas of psychology, management development, sales, marketing, and human factors engineering. It is a synthesis of concepts drawn from research in neuropsychology, linguistics, cognition, and anthropology.

One of the basic tenets of NLP is that each of us filters our communication and thinking in systematic and learnable ways. What Grinder and Bandler discovered is that this filtering process occurs through the use of our senses. That is, each of us has a preference for taking in information, organizing it "in our heads," and communicating information to others around us. This preference is based on the habitual and systematic use of our primary sense organs—literally, our eyes, ears, and body. Therefore, some of us prefer visual information—pictures, graphs, charts, memos, observing others, etc.; others may prefer auditory information—sounds, discussions, phone calls, voicemail, etc.; and some of us may prefer kinesthetic information—feelings, body language, face to face discussions, and physical movement and touching.

Thus, in the most general sense, each of us has either a visual, auditory or kinesthetic orientation to communication and thinking. We use ALL of our senses—however, the original NLP model predicts that we have an unconscious preference for using one sensory modality over another at any given time. The diagram below shows the original visual, auditory, and kinesthetic (or VAK) model of communication preferences.

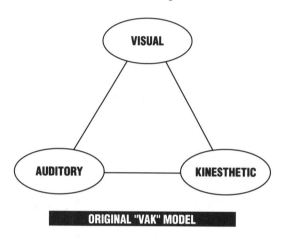

NLP: A New Paradigm For Understanding Communication Style

The model presented in *Making The Message Clear* is an enhancement over the original NLP theory and provides a complete, practical model of communication and change. In addition to the original NLP theory, it includes concepts from left/right brain neurological research, information processing models of cognition, and theories of adult learning.

Each of us has habitual ways of communicating. These "habits" of communication, or what I term your communication style, can be analyzed along three dimensions: how you take in information (i.e., attend to it)—your preferred sensory modality; how you organize information in your mind—your preferred thinking style; and how you express the information you receive to others—your preferred mode of expression.

The first two dimensions, when clustered together, represent your overall method of comprehension: the third dimension represents your overall method of production. Comprehension and production are key concepts from the fields of linguistics and cognitive psychology, and differentiate NLP-based communication, management, and sales models from other more traditional behavioral models based on "grid" matrices, e.g., social style and situational leadership. In order to develop successful communication practices, it is necessary to understand both the cognitive and behavioral processes involved.

Below you will find a communication style model that is a refinement of traditional "input/output" models and makes use of recently developed cognitive and behavioral concepts.

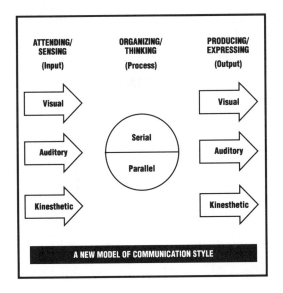

The Bottom Line

Research by Grinder, Bandler and many others has revealed that high achieving individuals are usually adept at recognizing or diagnosing another individual's communication style and then adapting to fit that style. This requires versatility or flexibility on the part of the high achiever, and the ability to synchronize with another individual's communication preferences. In the Neurolinguistic model of communication, this is termed "pacing."

Developing communication style fit and flexibility increases both the amount and accuracy of the information you exchange. This exchange, or reciprocity, is the foundation of your work relationships. If reciprocity is enhanced, rapport, trust, and achievement of work-related goals will increase, permitting you to lead others to mutually beneficial outcomes.

Successful communication demands fitting your style to match another's style and becoming flexible in your communication and thinking. Most importantly, learning the communication skills necessary to improve fit and style flexibility facilitates your important business transactions.

The following pages provide the reader with an introduction to many of these new, exciting and powerful communication tools!

James Eicher
Sunnyvale, California
Winter, 1993

Introduction

Communicating and the Importance of Making The Message Clear

"The unwritten rules of personal communication . . . occupy an amazing amount of company time. But take them away and no one would know how to behave. They let people know where they stand, reinforce an individual's identity within the company, and set the tone for the way in which people relate to one another . . . these rituals of social exchange govern relationships between bosses and workers, old and young, professionals and support staff, men and women, insiders and outsiders. They specify how formally or informally individuals are addressed, the long-standing customs that govern conversation, how much emotion or public controversy is permitted, who speaks first in meetings, and even who is permitted to end a conversation."

Deal and Kennedy (1982), *Corporate Cultures*, pp. 64-65.

The premise of this book is that there is *no excellence in management without excellence in communication.* Clear communication is necessary for both a corporation and an individual to be effective and productive. Excellent communication can solve work-related problems; poor communication is often the cause of similar problems.

On a one-to-one basis, managers and employees need to

communicate effectively so that tasks are clearly defined and work goals are understood by all parties involved. In order for a manager's organization to function efficiently, with good employee morale and high productivity, clear communication is an indisputable necessity.

The problem with becoming an effective communicator nee manager is a difficult one. We often know when communication "goes wrong," but what makes it go right? What are the learnable guidelines which distinguish inefficient, unproductive communication from efficient, productive communication?

In the following two sections, I discuss some working guidelines for communicating which will serve as a context or "backdrop" for the tools provided in this book. The two guidelines have to do with *rules* of communicating and communicating *intention*. Knowing about rules and intention in communication is the first step in learning to make the message clear.

Guideline One: Communication And Rules

Behavior is rule-governed. If you break employees' communication rules, confusing, unproductive behavior can follow. If you *intentionally* break rules of communication, the result may be humorous or may solve difficult business problems. If you break rules *unintentionally*, however, communication becomes unclear and, in the long run, unproductive.

There is a corollary to this: it's impossible not to communicate. Everything you do—the way you sit, fold your arms, use your tone of voice—is all some kind of communication and is thus the expression of a rule of communication.

One of the sets of rules about communication and behavior is the set about *verbal* communication—about language and how sentences are formed. For example, if I say, "John and Mary are nice," and you are fluent in English, you will recognize this as a correct or proper sentence and think nothing of it. However, if I say, "And John Mary nice are," chances are you might have a startled or peculiar reaction. You would be forced to "think" about the sentence (or non-sentence) and may, at first, have difficulty understanding it. If you look at the second sentence, what is peculiar about it is that an English language rule about word order has been broken. As a result, the communication may break down, be misinterpreted, or not be understood at all. Even though you don't normally think about rules of communication (that is, think in the sense of being conscious or aware), you do have a "sense" of when things go wrong. This "sense" is what is normally called intuition. You often become aware of the rules when they're broken. So, at some level of thinking, you do know some rules of communication, at least most of those for English. But if I say to you, "Haben sie eine zimmer frei?" you will not know if this is a proper sentence or even a sentence at all unless you know the rules of the German language. You have no "intuition" about this sentence. Is it correct? What is the message? You might not even know what language it is, and therefore you wouldn't know which rules of which language to apply.

Nonverbal communication also has rules. In some cases, it is most obvious when a nonverbal rule of communication is broken and trouble ensues. For example, if you are in a crowded movie theatre, you don't stand up in your seat during the movie and block other people's views. There is an unspoken, nonverbal rule of communication and behavior in that context that will be noticed if you violate it.

Similarly, if you are at a corporate board meeting, it may be customary for everyone to remain standing until the chief executive officer arrives and either sits down first or remains standing and gives a verbal or nonverbal cue to everyone else to be seated. If you were to sit down "out of turn," you would violate an unspoken rule of communication. Many possible messages and/or interpretations could be made from your violation of a nonverbal rule.

Often, the result of breaking a nonverbal rule is experienced as embarrassment or a sense of "not fitting in." Not following nonverbal rules of communication sends a signal to the rest of the corporate culture that you do not fit in—and the result can be rejection.

Another set of rules to consider is that of *politeness conventions*. These can be quite humorous if broken and are most obvious when they are. Politeness conventions embrace all types of behavior and vary from country to country, corporation to corporation, and individual to individual. What is important about these rules is that they usually combine verbal and nonverbal behaviors. They are a bit more complicated, but, like many rules of communication, are taken for granted until they are broken.

If I walk up to you and reach forward with a handshake, I will expect a similar nonverbal response—that you will also reach toward me with a handshake. But in conjunction with this, I usually express (and expect to receive back) an accompanying verbal greeting such as "Hi, how are you?" or "Good to see you." Now, imagine walking up to someone at work and simply exchanging handshakes with no words spoken at all. Many people would have an intuitive feeling that this was a bit strange—and the interaction could be interpreted as negative, positive, or in-between.

When rules of communication, such as politeness conventions, are broken intentionally, they are often very funny. Various forms of humor and comedy are nothing more than breaking rules of politeness conventions and their component patterns of verbal and nonverbal communication. So-called "slapstick" comedy is an example. In most of the Western world, it is customary to eat most foods with some type of utensil. However, it is not uncommon in a slapstick comedy for one of the characters to eat the food with his hands as a type of vulgar gag.

In the corporate arena, breaking rules of communication unintentionally can be humorous, at times. More often than not, however, being unaware of communication rules can be disastrous for individual employees, departments, and the corporation as a whole. Knowing your company's unspoken rules of communication is the first step in developing clear, productive communication. Putting rules of communication into action can create well-implemented corporate policies, trust and rapport in employees, and reduce the "hitches" which often occur when carrying out your day-to-day tasks.

Guideline Two: Communication And Intention

When people label someone's communication as good or bad, they are usually confusing the communicator's intention with their on-going communication. Your communication is not necessarily good or bad in a moral sense. However, as a communicator, you may do a poor job of conveying your intentions. As the old saying goes, "the road to hell is paved with good intentions"—and if I may modify the saying somewhat, the road to managerial hell is paved with good intentions and poor communication. Many times, your intentions are positive, but because of a lack of communicational finesse, your communication does not properly convey your positive intentions. When an employee judges you, he does not think about what your intentions might be. He responds to the overt, observable communication.

Many times when you sense that someone has had a bad day at the office, you may have the positive intention of "making them feel better." You may communicate this positive intention in one of two ways. You may either say to yourself, "Well, I'll leave him alone and let him blow off some steam or let him work it out for himself." Or you may decide to talk it out with him so that he doesn't "stew over it." But what if the person in question needs consoling and you leave him alone? Or, he needs to be left alone and you proceed to counsel him? He will make a judgement about you based not on your positive intention to make him feel better, but on your fitting or not fitting his particular needs. He may say to himself, "Gee, that Max sure is a meddler. I wish he'd just leave me alone. I need to think this out for myself." Or possibly, "I really need someone to talk to about this problem. Max is never around to talk to when I need him. He's so cold and insensitive."

This is a case where one person's good intentions were not properly conveyed to a fellow worker. Thus, judgement about a person was based on his communication and behavior. The important thing to note is that neither the intention nor the communication was bad. The employee, on the receiving end, simply confused Max's intention with his poor execution of communication. Max, for his part, was not astute enough to know how to properly convey his intention. By being aware of the difference between intention and communication, you avoid incorrect personal judgements about people and organizations that are ill-conceived and can lead to bad feelings, poorly executed tasks, low morale, and low productivity.

By focusing on personal communication as the expression of an individual's communication *rules* and not necessarily the expression of their *intention*, you can allow your management skills to develop without cumbersome "mental blocks" or "knee-jerk" reactions. The excellent manager can separate intentions from "people problems" and be able to cultivate an employee's talents more fully.

In summary, knowing about rules is important because it forces you to look at the process, the "how-to's" of communication. This will increase your ability to respond effectively in a changing business environment.

Knowing about intention is important because it forces you to look at work-related goals and outcomes. This will enable you to exercise increased control over the direction of your business environment—but not at the expense of employee morale and productivity.

Communicating With Style

1

The Basic Components of Communication

The simplest definition of communication is that it is "the sending and receiving of messages." It can be as simple as a common greeting ("Hello, how are you today?") and a response to that message. Responses are not only externally observable behaviors, such as a smile or a handshake. You experience many types of internal responses, as well, which can *generate* observable communication. If I say, "Hello," to you and you smile in return, that might make me feel good inside and cause me to smile. Thus, communication includes both "outside" *and* "inside" phenomena.

What do we mean by messages? Messages are the representation and exchange of *information*. How you think about things, the kind of sensory information you prefer, and the kinds of tasks you choose to do will influence how a message is received and responded to. You will learn in this chapter that a lot of things you do and don't do are dependent upon the communication patterns that you have learned over time.

In the work place, you often find certain tasks easier to accomplish than others. You might find that not only are there certain people that you get along with better than others, but also that some people are easier to work with and to successfully complete tasks with. There are patterns to the messages you've learned—and by learning the patterns, you can (1) learn more about what you do best, and worst; (2) learn how to improve your weak areas; and (3) learn to influence others in a mutually beneficial way.

This approach to learning communication is what I term "recognition-response." You need to first recognize the patterns of communication of yourself and those around you. Next, you need to know how to respond, how to develop as many options as possible. Finally, learning to recognize patterns of communication and learning to generate responses leads to control and adequate feedback regarding work situations. Having some control over your responses and reactions presupposes that you, as a manager or employee, can give and receive corrective feedback about your job, tasks, and long-term business strategies. All this leads to the creation of excellent, pro-active management—that is, "reading and feeding" to make the message clear.

Success or failure in the business environment ultimately depends on your awareness, your responsiveness, and the effectiveness of your communication.

Communication Style

Every musician, quarterback, dancer, writer, or newscaster has a particular style or way of doing things that is unique—in spite of the fact that they are all doing something that many other people do. So it is with communicating.

Everybody has a style of communicating that is unique to them and that allows them to both blend in *and* be different. When you have problems communicating, you're going to discover that you are experiencing a clash of communication styles; not a disagreement over the content so much, but friction over the style or process of communicating. You are also going to discover that you get along with people who have similar communication styles.

Have you ever made a "checklist" to compare yourself with someone else, writing down your religious backgrounds, political attitudes, favorite recreational activities, favorite books, etc.? After the lists are done are compared, it seems as though you will get along beautifully with the other person. Then, as you get to know him, you find you can't stand him.

You may also have had the opposite experience. You may have a totally different background from another person, you don't dress the same, you don't like the same kinds of movies, you don't vote for the same party, etc. It appears as if you wouldn't get along with that person, as you are as different as you could possibly be—and yet you get along wonderfully. This indicates the power of process over content in behavior.

What differentiates the second example is a similar style of communicating. Your process of communicating is very much the same, even if your individual opinions differ.

This explains how people in large corporations manage to get along and produce a product or service. Even though backgrounds and ideals are diverse, communication styles are merged sufficiently to achieve a mutually beneficial goal.

When you don't understand an employee's communication style and you break a communication rule, or when you make an incorrect assumption about an employee's communication and intention, that's when things go wrong. Now, let's explore how to make them go right.

Preferred Sensory Modality (PSM)

The first aspect of communication style is "preferred sensory modality" or PSM. Each person you work with has a preferred sensory modality or channel that influences their communication, a literal preference related to their eyes, ears, and body; seeing, hearing, and feeling.

Richard Bandler and John Grinder, the co-developers of Neurolinguistic Programming,[1] first developed the idea of preferred sensory modality for use in communication. In an article on their work, psychologist Dan Goleman (1979) sums up their idea as follows:

"By habit, and especially under stress, people rely on a favored sensory mode to gather information about the world, organize it, and express themselves. For this reason, knowing a person's favored mode and speaking to him or her in those terms can give a person a sense that his or her inner world is understood."

People Who Read People, pp. 69-71.

For example, if you are a *visually*-oriented person, you pay attention primarily to what you see. When someone asks you to think about something, you may experience it as looking at pictures in your mind's eye, or going to the movies in your head. You use phrases such as "that looks good" or "that's clear to me" or "that's a bright idea."

Auditorily-oriented people pay attention most to what they hear. They like verbal directions and enjoy listening to music and good conversations. Auditory people use phrases such as "that sounds good to me" or "let that rattle around in my head" or "that idea clicks for me."

Finally, some people pay attention primarily to feelings. There are two ways to think about feelings. You may pay attention to internally experienced feelings (*kinesthetic/visceral* experiences). You are very aware of your emotions at a "gut" level. You use phrases such as "I can get in touch with that" or "that feels good to me" or "I have a firm opinion." The other way is paying attention to externally experienced feelings or sensations (*kinesthetic/tactile* experiences). You notice how a chair feels physically against your back, your legs, and neck when you sit down.

All this may seem trivial. However, if you put someone who uses a primarily kinesthetic mode with someone who functions in a visual mode, you will have a clash of styles. One person will talk about feelings and another talk about pictures, and there will be a reduced exchange of information.

The following scenario is very common. After a program review meeting or presentation, the presenter asks his boss, "Well, George, how did the presentation *sound*?" Sitting in his seat, George is thinking, "You know, that *seat* was so *uncomfortable* that I really didn't pay attention to what he was *saying* at all." If you're in a meeting and your PSM is kinesthetic/tactile, then something as trivial as an uncomfortable chair might affect you. Visually-oriented people can't stand it if they can't see something. If they come to a meeting late and are forced to sit in the back of the room, or someone blocks their view, they may not pay attention to the content of the presentation.

There are two aspects of PSM to consider. The first is *external* sensory experience—what you see, feel, and hear "out there." The other pattern is your *internal* representation of sensory experience. Do you experience seeing images in your head or mind's eye? Do you experience feelings at a gut level that you're aware of? Do you experience talking to yourself (having an internal dialogue)?

People have internal dialogues in their heads all the time. They are asked to think about something, such as a problem at work, and they have a conversation with themselves while they're driving home. Many people also make pictures in their head or "mind's eye." Many people churn things over in their stomach—this is evidence of a kinesthetic/visceral pattern.

These are indicative of your *internal* PSM—which may or may not match your external PSM.

These seemingly minor patterns matter as far as how you think about things. They help form your reactions to people and your judgements about work and work-related tasks. Many times you have no idea why you thought a particular way. What you're aware of is your reaction. However, if you know the patterns that underlie your reaction, you have the tools to change · your pattern for optimum performance.

We often get into trouble in communicating and work when we violate some kind of communication rule. What you can learn from this book is what's beneath *expressing* those rules and patterns. Once you recognize what your communication style is, then you can learn to recognize someone else's communication style. This is the first step in solving any work-related problem.

Sample Case 1: The "Seeing I" Manager

One of the most concrete examples of miscommunication is when tasks are assigned and directions given.

A common pattern is when your boss likes tasks written down (visual preference) and you like to explain them verbally (auditory preference). You're not used to writing things down, or graphing them, or putting information onto milestone charts, or providing any of that kind of *visual* information. But the manager is used to receiving information and evaluating performance based on that modality.

A manager I once knew in a large corporation had a communication rule that she was completely unaware of. Her rule was, "If it's not written down, it's not real." Specifically, if tasks were not *visually* presented (written down) on a company memo that could be seen, then it didn't count. If she had an employee in a department who didn't like to write things down and preferred to have verbal exchanges, what kind of outcome could be expected? Anything from management/employee friction to a clash of communication styles and accompanying views of performance.

Excellent communication happens when you adjust your style to fit another's style. In the above case, one employee I knew intuitively realized the manager's rule about written visual information. He responded by expressing his weekly progress reports in written memo form. The result—a promotion over other employees in the department who had equal skill, experience, and education. What was potentially a vicious clash of styles became solvable. In a case like this, you might think to yourself, "That manager really likes things written down, so I'm going to make an effort to write more things down and present information visually." You're going to have to change a bit, but your work will be easier and more productive in the long run. Productivity will increase because information and goals will be communicated in a mutually acceptable way. This "matching of styles" is part of a problem-solving technique which will be discussed in more detail in Chapter 2.

In general, the more you know about communication (your own and other people's), the more *response*-able you are. Your *ability to respond* and change expands based on your increase in knowledge. Whether a subordinate or superior, the person who adjusts his communication is the one who is the most knowledgeable.

Preferred Thinking Style (PTS)

The second behavior pattern that influences communication style is the overall organization of thinking, your preferred thinking style (PTS).[2]

There are two generalized patterns of thinking. Some people have a tendency to be unsystematic and to pay more attention to general ideas and concepts. Some people have the tendency to be very detailed and systematic in their thoughts and actions. The former group will be labeled "big picture" people, visionary, or creative; the latter, "bean counters" or good organizers.

Another way of labeling these thinking patterns is *serial* and *parallel* processing. People who are detail-oriented and systematic tend to be serial thinkers who enjoy performing tasks in a step-by-step fashion. In business contexts, they want to complete one task before moving on to the next. Parallel process thinkers are inattentive to detail and do many work-related tasks at once, but complete them at inconsistent intervals.

Many jobs require a combination of these skills. However, most people find one pattern of organizing their thinking easier than another. This helps to explain why some people find a detail-oriented occupation such as accounting difficult or easy, or a strategic planning job that requires the ability to think about the "big picture" as easy or difficult.

Another term for information-processing is "chunking." Chunking refers to the amount of information you take in, process, and subsequently output. For example, employees who are serial thinkers usually chunk small. They carve tasks into small, detailed units of information. They might look at a report and note typos and grammatical errors. An employee who is a parallel thinker chunks larger. He might read a report and make comments on the overall theme and flow of thought.

The major application of PTS in business is in the sequencing of tasks, whether the tasks are visual, auditory, or kinesthetic in nature. Managers should think about whether an employee does tasks best in a step-by-step singular fashion, or in a multi-stepped, plural fashion. This may affect certain jobs an employee does well, and thus the manager's delegation of tasks and projects.

Here is a summary of the aspects of serial and parallel thinking:

Characteristics of Serial Processing
- attention to detail
- focusing on a single task
- performing tasks in a step-by-step fashion
- completing one task before moving on to the next
- ability to construct logical, step-by-step analyses
- colloquial expressions are *bean counter;*
  stickler for detail; well-organized.

Characteristics of Parallel Processing
- inattention to detail
- focusing on several tasks at once
- performing in a multi-task fashion
- completing tasks at inconsistent intervals
- ability to perform multi-leveled analyses
- colloquial expressions are *big picture person;*
  visionary; scattered.

An analogy of the difference between the two processes is comparing a blueprint of a design to a sketch. A blueprint is a much more detailed representation, and much closer "in time" to the actual manufacturing process. A sketch, on the other hand, is a very general, undetailed representation, far from the manufacturing process.

Sample Case 2: The Housing Tract

Instances of serial and parallel processing may have many applications outside the office as well. Let's consider the building of a home versus the building of a housing tract.

The custom home is built in a strictly serial fashion. Resources are allocated for only that house and its completion time is not necessarily dependent on the other homes adjacent to it. As a result, both labor and material costs are higher, and so is the price of the house.

When a contractor is building a housing tract, he is using both serial and parallel processing in the allocation of resources and construction of the project. In this situation, the combination of serial and parallel processes makes sense from a variety of labor, financial, and marketing points of view.

When constructing a housing tract, the homes are built in a specific sequence (serially), in phases which indicate thought-out, preplanned serialization. They are also in effect built in a parallel fashion. Each home is not completed one-at-a-time before the next is begun. Rather, the homes are constructed in parallel with other homes which were begun before the first was completed. Thus, you have an example of both serial and parallel processes.

Such a combination of processes underlies any effective manufacturing operation. When either of them breaks down or is not well thought-out, financial chaos can soon follow. In the case of the housing tract, the combination of serial and parallel processes allows for advanced planning, reduced labor costs, and purchase of building materials at a bulk rate.

There are occasions when a contractor builds several "custom homes" in an area at approximately the same time. But even though the homes are not usually adjacent to one another and their completion times are not coordinated as closely as the tract home, this type of construction still represents a more serial approach.

Processes such as home construction follow the patterns of thinking styles. These thinking styles, like the other patterns discussed so far, are powerful, conspicuous behaviors in the day-to-day lives of managers and employees. And like all patterns of communication style, if the rules a person or project or organization has about thinking are broken, disaster can soon follow. If a strike or shortage of material interrupts the serial/parallel construction of a housing tract, the developer can literally lose his shirt. The successful contractor knows intuitively that integrating these concepts into the actual planning and implementation of construction increases profitability through superior manpower and planning.

"Piling It On"

The idiomatic expression, "piling it on," refers to delegating a lot of work in a short period of time. People who perform well when work is piled on are those that have both serial and parallel abilities well integrated. They can sort out multi-levels of material and organize the "mess" into a step-by-step sequence. Thus, the power of good delegation relies in part on knowledge of thinking styles and then implementing the knowledge for effective task delegation.

Exercise 1

Answer the following questions as honestly and accurately as possible. Check **one** box only for each question.

1. While attending a movie, I become most annoyed when:
   A ❐ The picture is fuzzy, scratchy, or out of focus;
   B ❐ The sound is too loud, too low, or of poor quality;
   C ❐ The seats are uncomfortable, filthy, or too close together to allow sufficient leg or shoulder room.

2. What I do most often to relax after a long, difficult day is to:
   A ❐ Watch a movie or television; read a book or magazine;
   B ❐ Listen to music or talk with a close friend or relative;
   C ❐ Engage in a recreational sport such as tennis, golf or basketball or take a hot bath or shower.

3. If given a choice about filling out long, detailed forms such as tax forms, I would much rather:
   A ❐ Fill them out myself;
   B ❐ Have someone else fill them out.

Now go back to questions 1 and 2 and rank them according to preference.

Questions 1 and 2 give you an idea of your preferred sensory modality (PSM) (A = visual, B = auditory, C = kinesthetic).

Question 3 gives you an idea of your preferred thinking style (PTS) (A = serial, B = parallel).

This exercise is not a definitive diagnostic survey. It is meant to serve as a "prompt" to get you to think about the different information processing preferences that you have.

Preferred Modes of Expression (PME)

There's a third set of patterns that affect your communication style: *expression variables.* In addition to the two sets of information processing factors, you have a set of adjunct patterns, your preferred modes of expression (PME). Expression variables are just that—components of your communication that you can change or vary for different outcomes. They are patterns of personal expression which differentiate you from other people, and they are very powerful in that they often subliminally affect the behavior of other people.

Most employees and managers tend to use one mode of expression over another to influence other people's behavior. For example, you may use your tone of voice, facial expressions, gestures, or eye contact to express your thoughts and feelings. Most of the time, you're unaware of your own patterns. However, these are powerful tools which you can consciously use to secure mutually beneficial outcomes and create a "good mood" which often goes hand in hand with high employee productivity. It is the "feed" side of the "read and feed" method.

The variables that make up your expression style fall into verbal and nonverbal categories, the verbal messages being augmented by nonverbal ones. Some of the more important modes of expression are outlined as follows.

Verbal Patterns

■ Word Usage
There are certain *categories* of individual words that people have *usage* rules about, those that you can and can't use, and most of the time you're unaware of these rules. For example, some

people don't like swear words. If every other word you use is an expletive, fellow employees might have a positive or negative reaction. Some people feel alienated by technical words. You need to be aware of usage patterns and the positive or negative responses people have to word categories.

One of the most powerful word categories is that which indicates a person's PSM or *representational system*. These are the categories of visual, auditory, and kinesthetic words. They are useful for a variety of communication needs such as specifying the type of information you need for a particular assignment (e.g., visual information such as charts and graphs, auditory information such as a phone call, etc.). The following is a brief list of sensory-oriented words:

visual	*auditory*	*kinesthetic*
clear	sound	feel
bright	hear	touch
see	roar	pressure
look	intone	push
flash	loud	handle
color	verbalize	move
view	say	guts
envision	speak	fondle

■ Grammatical Style

Another verbal pattern that is important to understand is grammatical style. Suppose someone is smoking and you want them to stop. You could say, "Excuse me, I have a problem with smoke." Notice that that's a statement as opposed to an order or a question. This is a part of politeness conventions. There is a big difference between making a statement such as "I have trouble with smoke" and an order such as, "Put that thing out!" An order elicits a very different reaction. Oftentimes, you label someone's behavior and your relationship to them based on their grammatical style. You might label a person who uses a lot of orders as "bossy" or "authoritarian." Or you might label someone who uses a lot of statement or declarations as "absolutist" or "stuffy."

The main categories of grammatical style to be aware of are

Orders ("Stop that!"), **Statements** ("I want you to stop that"), and **Questions** ("Would you please stop that?"). Each form will elicit a different response from fellow employees. There are times when one style is more appropriate and effective than another.

■ Metaphors

Many people use metaphors and imagery when they're describing or explaining things. One common pattern in the United States is the use of sports metaphors, such as "sliding home" or "it's a triple" or "it's a grand slam." People often use football or hockey or basketball phrases. A management team may describe going after a competitor as "putting on a full court press." Many people who are familiar with computer science or information science use a lot of computer metaphors. They use terms such as "up-time" and "down-time" to describe their moods ("I need down-time" or "I'm experiencing a glitch in my thinking").

The main distinction between individual word usage and metaphor is that metaphors and imagery are usually used to describe ongoing processes. You will discover that every department, whether it's finance, marketing, engineering, accounting, purchasing, etc., has its own technical imagery and metaphors. And it is *absolutely crucial* for successful management to learn the metaphors and imagery of an organization and use them when expressing your goals. Metaphors are powerful tools for initiating change.

Nonverbal Patterns Which Augment Verbal Behavior

■ Voice Quality

The nonverbal communication patterns which *augment* verbal behavior can be the pitch, tone, inflection, volume, or accent of someone's voice; that is, the overall voice *quality*.

Suppose an employee is speaking to you in a whining tone. You may have a negative reaction which is not based on their ability to perform tasks but on their voice quality. Suppose a manager has an assignment for you. You go into his office, sit down and ask in a loud, angry tone, "What do you want?" You may not make the best impression on your manager.

Most of us have been on the opposite end of a pleasant, even seductive tone of voice which influences our actions as well!

If you speak very slowly, like "syrup," fellow employees may have a negative reaction to that. They might experience wanting to "pull the words out of your mouth." They might get bored or impatient, or some might think it was humorous or relaxing.

Certain inflections that people use are associated with region, and an accent can affect your response to someone. Sometimes it depends on how thick the accent is (that's a good kinesthetic term—thick!)

In general, voice quality can be used to influence action and create either excellent or poor rapport with fellow employees.

Nonverbal Patterns of Movement

Movement includes both gross movement and small movements such as those of eye contact, head turning, etc. Often what people call "vibes" or "demeanor" will be related to the patterns discussed in this section.

■ Gestures

People have rules about gestures. Some people are easily distracted by rapid arm and hand motions. Others find it entertaining, as it keeps their attention. In certain situations, such as meetings, it is not proper to use some arm or hand gestures. (Now think about professional comics. A comic act is often a series of exaggerated, mocking, or perhaps vulgar gestures.) Excellent use of gestures can often motivate employees and excite them about tasks and projects.

■ Posture

Suppose a manager you know was chairing a meeting, and during the entire meeting he slouched over, or sat extremely stiffly. After a while, you may (or may not) notice that you began slouching or stiffening yourself. You may come away with a negative reaction to a meeting or presentation, not because of *what* was said, but because of the posture of the speaker. A dynamic speaker uses posture to influence the response of the audience.

■ Facial Expression

A great deal of communication is conveyed through facial expression and changes in expressions. If an employee's face is screwed-up or has an exaggerated look to it, you could have a variety of responses to that expression. You may have interacted with someone who has a perpetual frown on their face. They always look unhappy, and you often *internalize* it.

One of the biggest errors people make in communication is misinterpreting facial expressions. Someone could be very intently thinking about something and you might think they are angry or pensive. You can reach a lot of conclusions about someone based on incorrect interpretations of facial expression.

Many times you are unaware of the expressions on your own face. People key off them, and you can get a negative response or be misinterpreted. On the positive side, well-executed facial expressions enhance interactions and can "make people feel good" about themselves and their jobs.

■ Eye Contact

Many people have strict rules about eye contact. If someone came into your office and walked around, looking down, and never made eye contact with you, you might try to somehow force their eyes up. Some internal rules that people have about eye contact might be, "She's not looking at me; she's not listening to me," or "He's not looking at me, he's not paying attention; he doesn't understand." Know what *your* rules are, and be aware of other people's needs for eye contact. Give them contact if they need it.

Reading eye contact correctly and giving it back properly enhances communication and helps establish good rapport. Eye contact is a powerful tool in and of itself for you as a manager. If used correctly, it can indicate trust, understanding, and approval.

Nonverbal Patterns of Space And Time

■ Space and Touching

The next expression variable refers to rules about *spatial* communication. People have many rules about space, and these rules have to do with physical closeness and/or touching *and* physical orientation or position. Everyone has rules about how close people can be, depending upon the relationship. If you violate spatial rules, you get various kinds of reactions.

An idiomatic expression that illustrates this concept is to "give someone room to maneuver." Two meanings can be gathered from this saying. A psychological meaning is to allow someone their beliefs and attitudes. There is also a literal meaning. If you observe that an employee begins to look uncomfortable when you're only a few feet away, and conversely begins to breathe and look relaxed when you're farther away, then you know something about his rules about spatial relationships.

You will see this a lot in business meetings. When someone walks into a room, depending on who's there and the rank of the people, everyone jockeys for position. The employees are positioning themselves in the room in order to control the forthcoming communication.

Rules about touching are an extension of rules about space. It's permissible to touch some people on the shoulder or knee in casual conversation, but in other cases, it's not permissible. An example is a conversation between two American businesspeople. Standing side by side, it may be permissible to give each other a slap or pat on the back, even if they are not from the same company. However, in Saudi Arabia, there are very strict rules about certain kinds of touching. Such a slap on a sheik's back may not only be seen as extremely rude, but may also destroy your chances of a business deal.

Anthropologists Edward Hall and William Whyte (1960) offer yet another example of rules about touching in a multicultural setting:

"... there are cultures which restrict physical contact far more than we do. An American at a cocktail party in Java

tripped over the invisible ropes which mark the boundaries of acceptable behavior. He was seeking to develop
a business relationship with a prominent Javanese and
seemed to be doing very well. Yet, when the cocktail
party ended, so apparently did a promising beginning.
For the North American spent nearly six months trying to
arrange a second meeting. He finally learned, through
pitying intermediaries, that at the cocktail party he had
momentarily placed his arm on the shoulder of the
Javanese—in the presence of other people. Humiliating!
Almost unpardonable in traditional Javanese etiquette."

Intercultural Communication, pp. 295-296.

■ Time

Rules about time are very powerful and, if understood and
used properly, can make or break a business deal. Again Hall and
Whyte offer an excellent example of the effect of time on the
"business deal":

"The head of a large, successful Japanese firm com-
mented: You Americans have a terrible weakness. We
Japanese know about it and exploit it every chance we
get. You are impatient. We have learned that if we just
make you wait long enough, you'll agree to anything."

Intercultural Communication, p. 297.

Thus, it is crucial that you have an awareness of your own
rules about time as well as those of others. The effect of knowing
rules about time and using "time pressure" is very powerful,
particularly in the context of negotiation.

Ethnicity In Communication

An employee's ethnic background will often dictate what
kind of rules he has about communication. In America, where
there is so much ethnic diversity, it helps to pay attention to all

different kinds of ethnically-oriented responses. This is how an individual often "packages" his communication—according to his ethnic background.

Consider the metaphor, "Italians talk with their hands." What this indicates is a particular nonverbal pattern that people have in that particular culture (they use their hands in a particular pattern in conjunction with their spoken language). Italians, Greeks and people in Mideastern cultures may employ similar gestural patterns.

Dr. Paul Watzlawick (1977) states that in regard to ethnic communication:

> "Members of any given society share myriads of behavior patterns that were 'programmed' into them as a result of growing up in that particular culture, subculture and family tradition, and some of these patterns may not have the same connotations to an outsider. The ethnologists tell us that there are literally hundreds of ways of, for instance, greeting another person or expressing joy or grief in different cultures."

and he continues by saying:

> "In every culture, there is a very specific distance that two strangers will maintain between each other in a face-to-face encounter. In Central and Western Europe and in North America, this is the proverbial arm's length, as the reader can easily verify by inviting any two people to walk up to each other and stop at the "right" distance. In Mediterranean countries and in Latin America, the distance is considerably shorter. Thus, in an encounter between a North American and a South American, both try to take up what they consider the right distance. The Latin moves up; the Northerner backs away to what he unconsciously feels is the proper distance; the Latin feeling uncomfortably distant, moves closer, etc. Both feel that the other is somehow behaving wrongly and try to "correct" the situation, creating a typical human prob-

lem in which the corrective behavior of one partner inspires a reverse correction by the other. And since in all probability there is nobody around who could translate their respective body languages for them . . . they will blame each other for their discomfort."

How Real Is Real?, p. 6-7.

Political events in the Mideast offer some of the most interesting examples of rules of communication. During the Camp David negotiations with Sadat, Begin, and Carter, in the 1970s, a contrast in greetings was clear. It is acceptable for two European or Mideastern men to greet each other with a ritualized kiss. People who watched the television media coverage saw that the Americans didn't refuse the gesture. They went along with the ethnic and cultural rule of communication—the spatial pattern of touching and proximity. But from their facial expression and postures, it appeared evident that the Americans were uncomfortable.

So here is an example of a ritualized communication pattern you would rarely see two American diplomats or businessmen doing, but which would be common for Europeans or Mideastern people. This example points out the obvious differences. The differences are much more subtle between people of the same culture (and more so between people from the same company), but the differences and accompanying rules exist nonetheless. They are another set of patterns you need to become aware of so that you can properly express yourself and achieve your business goals.

Exercise 2

Pick a business-related experience you had during the past week which you would label as productive or successful.

1. Review the list of expression variables, and;
2. Mentally review the selected experience and determine what

expression variable(s) influenced your labeling of the experience as productive. For example, did the individual(s) involved match your PSM and/or PTS? Were their voice quality, gestures, or posture an influence? Or eye contact?

Exercise 2 develops your awareness of and sensitivity to expression variables and how they influence the ways you interpret communication.

A good way to learn patterns of expression variables is to save a little time at the end of the work day and sit back and think about your interactions. In your mind, visualize, hear, and feel your interactions and/or replay the conversations that you had or some combination thereof. You will discover that you're learning many of these patterns intuitively. You may find yourself thinking, "When that person was talking in computerese, I started to talk back to him in computerese."

Summary

In this chapter, we covered the basic elements of communication style. Your communication style is a reflection of your rules (processes) about communication. It forms the building blocks for reading employees' behavior accurately and then giving appropriate feedback to obtain your desired goals. The major components of communication are:

1. **Preferred Sensory Modality (PSM)**
   Your preference to take in and represent information either primarily visually, auditorily, or kinesthetically;
2. **Preferred Thinking Style (PTS)**
   Your preference for organizing your thoughts and behavior in either a serial or parallel manner;
3. **Preferred Modes of Expression (PME)**
   The aspects of verbal and nonverbal communication you use to express yourself and influence others.

These three sets of patterns (see Figure 1) provide you, the manager/employee, with the basic tools needed to analyze yourself and others and then learn to change and influence behavior to get the job done better.

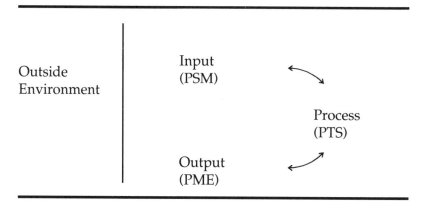

Figure 1

At the end of this chapter, you should be able to recognize aspects of your communication style such as:

- Preferred sensory modality (visual, auditory, kinesthetic);
- Preferred thinking style (serial, parallel);
- Preferred modes of expression (word usage, grammatical style, posture, eye contact, etc.).

Action Plan

Do the exercises in this chapter.

Devote 15 minutes each day (not necessarily in one increment) to observing aspects of your communication style and 15 minutes to observing aspects of others' communication styles.

Pick one work-related situation each day such as evaluating an employee, assigning a task, disagreeing with someone at a meeting, etc. Analyze the situation by asking yourself: (1) "How did my communication in this situation reflect my personal rules about communication?" (2) "Did I successfully communicate my intentions?"

Seeing Eye (I) To Eye (I)

2

Developing Strategies For Gaining Employee Empathy And Rapport

Developing Cognitive Strategies

Let's extrapolate on the idea of Preferred Sensory Modality (PSM). When you're paying attention to information "outside" of yourself, you're going to tend to pay attention to either visual, auditory, or kinesthetic information. Internally, you're also going to process and represent sensory information in chiefly one channel (what is referred to as "thinking"). That is, you're going to *experience* thinking more or less in pictures (in the "mind's eye"), with internal dialogue (talking to yourself), or as emotional, gut-level responses or physical reactions.

As mentioned before, your external and internal sensory experiences do not have to match. As a matter of fact, much of the time they won't. Rather, they will "cross-over" or overlap. Thus, you often have a PSM for representing your internal sensory experience which is different from that of your external sensory experience. Together, the two PSM's form your most elementary ways of perceiving and thinking.

For example, you may see something externally (such as watching a medical operation being performed) and then immediately have a gut level kinesthetic/visceral reaction. Or you may hear something externally (such as a child's voice) and then see a picture of what you hear in your "mind's eye." This elementary pattern is called a cognitive strategy.[1]

Cognitive strategies are combinations or sequences of your

external and internal PSM. They can be represented as follows: visual = V; auditory = A; kinesthetic = K; and external = e; internal = i.

If your preferred strategy in a given situation is seeing things externally and then having feelings about them, you could represent that as Ve -> Ki.

This way of representing PSM is meant to aid you in becoming aware of how people take information, internally process it, and output the information (See Figure 2). Knowing this will aid you in understanding and influencing other's perspectives and business needs. For example, for the manager who thinks in pictures, presenting him with data in a visual mode (graphs, charts, etc.) as opposed to an auditory mode (verbal reports) will be the most useful and appreciated method of communicating and getting the job done.

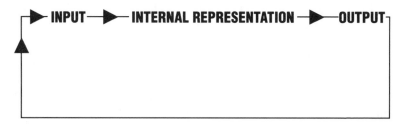

Figure 2

How do you know which internal sensory modality a person is using? You check his output or expression in two ways: verbal and nonverbal behavior, and habits.

Listen for the words that people use to describe their experience. Visual words (see, look, envision) indicate visual processing; kinesthetic words (feel, touch, handle) indicate kinesthetic processing; and auditory words (sound, hear, click) indicate auditory processing. Nonverbal expression can also indicate internal processes. For example, strong kinesthetic/visceral reactions may be revealed in tense body posture, an emotional tone of voice, or an animated facial expression. Visual processing may be represented by fixed eye contact on an object or person. And auditory processing may be indicated by foot-tapping to music or lack of eye contact accompanied by humming.

Cognitive strategies can also be indicated by an employee's habits (i.e., rules of communication). Some people primarily engage in physical activities for recreation, some go to movies, some enjoy music or dance. Personal habits also indicate internal and external strategies and give you a "handle" (so to speak) on how employees communicate and think.

The beauty of knowing cognitive strategies from a management point of view is that you will be able to orchestrate employee communication styles for maximum harmony and team effort. Another important function is developing your "rehearsal" strategies and enhancing your ability to think management problems through.

Sample Case 1: The Blind Doctor

This is a case where a doctor had a rule about eye contact. Dr. Max closed his eyes whenever he was asked a medical question. It's one think to look away or not to give somebody full eye contact; it's another to stand there and close your eyes. This is an obvious violation of rules about eye contact.

If you have a rule about needing eye contact, what's the potential outcome of this situation? The doctor could lose business by unintentionally offending his clientele. The potential is a loss of money from not being particularly observant of how to communicate and what someone else prefers.

From a communication style point of view, what could be going on with this doctor? As mentioned earlier, people often experience thinking by making pictures in their head. For some people, it's generally easier to make these pictures *with their eyes closed*. As the doctor listened to his client, he processed information in a way that he knew was best to diagnose her problem—in visual images. Thus, his *intention* was positive, but his communication may have been perceived as negative.

Ideally, if the doctor had been aware of his communication pattern, he might have addressed the client about it. He could say, "Excuse me, but I find that in order to think about your situation and give you the best diagnosis, I have to close my eyes and think about it very intently for a few seconds." With that statement, the client would probably feel relieved, and willing to *suspend* her rule about eye contact. This is one approach to take. Most people (but not all!) will understand a reasonable explanation of what you're doing in regard to communication. So if you do understand what you're doing, one option is to explain the cognitive strategy to others. Another option for Dr. Max would be to recognize his client's eye contact rule and respond by giving eye contact, thus establishing rapport.

When Dr. Max is listening, he's more than likely *listening* (auditory external preference) to the client's words *and* making a picture (visual internal preference) of what the client is telling him in order to diagnose her problem. He could be making pictures of her nose, bronchial tubes, lungs, etc. This strategy is a cross-over from auditory external to visual internal which can be represented as Ae->Vi.

Some people have a problem making pictures in their heads, and one of the ways that they concentrate is to literally shut out what they see "out there" so that they can see things better in their mind's eye. When you visualize, you might turn away or close your eyes because *cutting off the external stimulus* makes it easier to create a picture in your head. For the auditorily inclined, you can often think better (i.e., talk to yourself) when there's no sound around you. That is the *same* as the doctor closing his eyes, just in a different sensory modality.

The same is true of kinesthetics, people who think "physically." Often they're sitting and mulling over a problem or an argument, having all kinds of gut-level visceral feelings, or they're tactilely processing information, sitting in their chair, tapping their feet and/or the table. (Note: kinesthetic processing is often modified in business situations because there are strict rules about touching.)

Let's say you're at home with your spouse, and you're deep in thought about something when they come up and touch you. Or if you have kids, they run up and grab your leg. You might react as if you'd just had an electric shock. You're processing information kinesthetically, and the person interrupts the process by diverting your tactile sensory processing.

If you're sitting in your office, thinking, and an employee comes in and approaches within a certain physical range, it may interrupt your train of thought. This is a situation where someone does something that annoys you, and you don't quite know what it was. You only know that you were thinking in a certain way, and someone came in and interrupted you. As you further develop skills in applying cognitive strategies to business, your overall repertoire of communication strategies will grow.

Interpreting Communication Style

"Man communicates not by words alone. His tone of voice, his facial expressions, his gestures all contribute to the infinitely varied calculus of meaning. But the confusion of tongues is more than matched by the confusion of gesture and other culture cues. One man's nod is another man's negative."

Hall and Whyte (1960), *Intercultural Communication*, p. 294.

One way to accurately read people and further develop your communication strategies is to observe how they communicate when they are talking about a pleasant experience versus an unpleasant one.

When employees around you speak about a situation, listen for verbal patterns, phrases where they use metaphors, certain words, etc. Pay close attention to their tone of voice, tempo, inflection, and changes in their posture, gestures, and facial expressions.

You might find it very easy to listen to people, or easier to watch and to notice changes in gestures, etc. You might discover that you are so wrapped up in your own feelings that you neither see nor hear anyone else.

You can learn to calibrate verbal and nonverbal communication, whether positive or negative. This will assist you in interpreting and influencing your employees' communication patterns. The chart on the next page will also help.

	Positive Situation		Negative Situation	
	Person A	*Person B*	*Person A*	*Person B*
Your visual observation	smiles, is snimated	face is placid, little movement	scrunches face, tightens up	throws head back, grimaces
Your auditory observation	laughs out loud, stomps feet	quiets down	sobs, pounds fist	laughs shrilly, slaps thigh

You will notice changes in the behavior of the person you are observing. When they talk about a positive experience, their pitch may go up and they will sit up. While describing a negative experience, they will slouch, their pitch will drop, and they will take on a cranky tone of voice, etc.

Depending upon the person and the situation, and on whether the person is talking about a pleasant or unpleasant experience, there will be a general change in the pattern of communication. You will want to concentrate on patterns of variation in an individual's communication as it changes from positive to negative experiences. The variation and patterns aren't random. They occur with each and every individual according to certain situations, events, and topics in a fairly predictable way. When one person talks about a positive experience, he may speak slowly and another person may speak quickly. Often, one individual will do the opposite of another under exactly the same circumstances. For example, one person may laugh when under stress and cry in a happy one—another may cry in a stressful situation and laugh in a happy one. You will notice the differences in communication styles as indicated by the observable expression variables noted in Chapter 1.

Constantly misreading people's moods leads to morale-related productivity problems and actually creates problems where none may have existed. This is the "read" side. On the "feed" side, you can learn to give people positive reinforcement about their tasks, performance, etc., if you can make correct assessments of their communication style. The excellent manager is recognized as the one who says or does the right thing to the right employee at the right time. He has a communication strategy, the uncanny ability to read others and reinforce behavior in positive, productivity-boosting ways.[2]

If one employee associates speaking in a certain volume and a certain tempo with a positive experience, you know it's a pattern he has. You can then learn to make *better than random* assessments about whether he is talking about something that's important and positive to him. Similarly, if you learn what constitutes negative communication for him, you'll know whether what he's talking about is something that is bothering him. This is part of the process of learning to calibrate and reinforce employee communication for improved morale and productivity.

Paying attention to other people also tells you what your sensory preferences and limitations are. You'll see where your limitations get you into trouble and where your strengths lie. A lot of people don't pay attention to what other people say. On the other hand, they may get lots of information from nonverbal communication. Ultimately, what you want, as a more effective manager, is to exercise maximum variety in effectively dealing with communication impasses.

Exercise 3

While in a position to politely and unobtrusively observe a conversation, note:

1. If the people are discussing a positive or negative experience.;
2. If this is the case, then
   a. Listen for verbal patterns (words, imagery, voice quality) and;

b.Watch for nonverbal (gestures, facial expressions, posture) patterns and differences between the negative and positive experiences.

This exercise develops your ability to read another's communication styles and develop strategies to express constructive responses. A simple observational exercise such as this informs you of your patterns and limitations and the patterns and limitations of others.

"Telepathy" Versus "Sympathy"

In connection with observing others, a communication error occurs frequently. We commonly call it "sympathy" but it is more like "mind-reading." When you experience sympathy, you feel how *you* would feel in a similar situation as a colleague. You offer the response you would like in that situation. This is a process of thinking, decision-making and interpreting that just about everyone does. But, remember, you are feeling how *you'd* feel in that situation, and it may or may *not* be the way the other person is feeling. You may *think* it's the way the other person is feeling, but you don't know *exactly*. It's not that your intuitions are incorrect, it's just that when you try to project them back onto the other person, there's a good chance for inaccuracy and thus false assumptions that hinder good, clear communication.

Synchronizing Communication For Empathy And Rapport[3]

It's been mentioned that for some managers, it's extremely important for them to see an assignment written down or to have something they can hold in their hand for a message to really mean anything. You could be doing a million and one projects, but if you're not writing them down on some type of corporate memo or keeping a written (visual) record, they won't pay attention to what you're doing. Whether this is fair or efficient or inefficient is a separate matter. In the short run, if that's what your manager wants, that's what you do, even if that's not your preferred communication style. When you match someone else's style or mode, particularly when someone is very stubborn or resistant, that's a crucial step in actualizing your communication strategies for making positive changes. Conceptually, you are making a pro-active change by reducing or eliminating possible conflict.

Thus, the next step after learning communication styles is to learn to synchronize (match) communication styles to gain employee empathy and rapport and to begin to establish various kinds of strategic relationships. In order to establish rapport in face-to-face communication, you synchronize communication. At times, you'll want to match facial expressions, speech, movement, etc. For example, if someone is talking to you in "computerese," you're going to try to give them back some "computerese" to show you understand their point.

Not matching an employee's communication style is a crucial communication violation that can develop into business problems. This disrupts whatever task you're trying to do. At one time or another, you have probably met someone and have had a "sense" of not jibing with that person. This intuition is a consequence of mismatching behaviors with the person and thus not synchronizing communication styles.

Sample Case 2: The "Hot Under The Collar" Employee

Suppose an employee came into your office and seemed very angry with you over some company policy. Ideally, what you would want to do is to match them to a certain extent. This is where you have a fine line in establishing working rapport and trust. You only want a *partial* match of the employee's communication because if you match completely in a *crisis*, it may come across as mimicry—which gets different results than empathy.

For establishing empathy and rapport in a situation like this, first determine what part of the employee's behavior is out of control. Anger, in this case, is too general a description. Let's assume that his voice (specifically, the volume and pitch) is the part that's out of control. That's the part to leave alone (not match).

Now, what part is in control? Let's assume his posture is fairly normal. *That's* the part that is in control and the part you want to match.

Don't deal with what the employee is saying or how they're saying it right now. When you stand up and match posture, then sit down (the employee will follow), and take a deep breath and relax. The employee will also take a deep breath and start to relax. The pitch and volume of his voice will go down, and the tempo of his voice will slow. While *tracking* the employee's behavior, you can then start to talk to him about the specific problem. ("What's going on? What is the problem?") The employee, having experienced his anger, will be more reasonable. You, for your part, have shown great empathy and given him implicit support, all by becoming synchronized with him and tracking his emotional state.

In sum, in difficult or stressful situations, identify the expression variables in control and out of control, match the ones in control, and track the ones out of control. Then problem-solve.

The Mirroring Metaphor

When assisting employees in understanding or solving work-related problems, recognize that for some people, a rational explanation is not what they need in order to experience "understanding." If you're systematic, detailed, reasonable, and analytical (a serial thinker), that's the way *you're* going to think. A lot of people are frustrated rather than pacified by having concerns explained to them. It makes them more angry.

What the employee may need is *nonverbal* rapport-building as described above or they may need you to use verbal rapport-building, such as "Just between you and me, you're right. This is a poor policy." It may sound ridiculous, but for some people that's exactly what they need to hear. This is also a form of synchronism.

Ultimately, you have to decide what to do on an individual basis. You might say, "Look, when you've cooled down, come back and talk to me." Even said harshly, that might work for some employees.

To demonstrate a sense of rapport with employees, it is necessary to synchronize your behavior and in effect "mirror" the employee.

Consultant Michael McCaskey (1979) sums up the "mirroring metaphor" as follows:

> "In moments of great rapport, a remarkable pattern of nonverbal communication can develop. Two people will mirror each other's movements—dropping a hand, shifting their body at exactly the same time. This happens so quickly that without videotape or film replay, one is unlikely to notice the mirroring. But managers can learn to watch for disruptions in this mirroring because they are dramatically obvious when they occur. In the midst of talking, when a person feels that the other has violated his expectations or values, he or she will often signal distress. If norms or status differences make it unwise to express disagreement or doubt verbally, then the message will be conveyed through nonverbal "stumbles."
>
> Instead of smooth mirroring, there will be a burst of movement, almost as if both are losing balance. Arms and legs may be thrust out and the whole body posture changed in order to regain balance. Stumbles signal the need to renegotiate what's being discussed. The renegotiation occurs very rapidly and subtly and often through nonverbal channels. Managers who are aware of stumbles and what they mean have an option open to them that unaware managers do not. They can decide whether a given situation could be more effectively dealt with by verbally discussing it."

The Hidden Messages Managers Send, p. 147.

Mirroring behavior creates trust, empathy, rapport, and a special harmony of relations. *It is almost impossible to work effectively as a team without it.*

So here's Sam Supervisor, and you want to establish rapport with him. What is your communication strategy at this point?

First, you're going to scan him visually and auditorily, notice his posture, and stay in touch with your feelings so as to not get too nervous. However, you've just been hired, and you're going to be working for Sam, so you might be a little nervous. You want to relax and breathe and stay in touch with your feelings. To become synchronized, adopt his posture, gestures, facial expression, tone and tempo of voice, *and* you're going to pay attention to the words he's using to decide if he's speaking in visual, kinesthetic, or auditory words or metaphors. You're mirroring his overall behavior, and you track Sam's responses and monitor how synchronized his responses are to you.

If Sam's giving you eye contact, give him eye contact back. If he shakes his head up and down when he's listening and responding, you might want to do a little of that. The way you can tell it has a powerful impact is if you do the *opposite* of what he's doing. You can see, hear, and feel how really disconcerting and disorienting mismatched communication is (as noted by McCaskey).

Suppose someone comes into your office and instead of taking on your posture (relaxed, sitting easily in a chair), they did not pay any attention to you. They held a completely different posture, with their shoulders back and rigid, and they sat down and looked at the floor while you were speaking. How might you react?

Similarly, you may have intuitions about other people in your work environment. You often comment to yourself, "Well, I like this person, or I don't like this person, or they seem like they'd be good for this job." Those intuitions come from verbal and nonverbal communication, subliminally recognizing sensory information, and matching (mirroring) behavior—or not matching. The old cliche "seeing eye to eye" fits here.

Synchronizing For Decisions

Let's turn to the issues of decision-making, consensus, and the role of matching. Whether you reach a consensus or not, what's important is to be synchronized as far as your communication style, to have an indication of rapport and employee/

management support. It doesn't matter so much whether you agree or disagree on the *content*. What's important is to maintain the ongoing process of communication. It's one thing to disagree on something that you both understand you're disagreeing on. It's quite another thing to not even be able to communicate about it at all.

In work-related problems, it's much more important to be versatile with respect to communicating than it is to necessarily reach the same decision. When you get a team of people together who have fluid, synchronous communication styles, business projects will be solved easily. As long as there's communication between the people, there's a possibility of resolution.

The first step in problem-solving and decision-making is synchronizing your communication styles. Mirroring is part of doing that. If you wanted to put together a task force for a particular problem, you could have someone inside or outside the corporation intentionally do a support-building exercise which would synchronize the communication of the team. In a very short period of time, you would see a building of rapport and mutual support. The excellent manager creates a rapport-building environment so that decisions can be made effectively and rapidly.

Congruency And Clarity

One thing to avoid in communication is confusing and conflicting messages. Let's say an employee walks up to you and shakes his head from left to right while saying, "That's a really nice tie." He says with words that he likes your tie, but may also be saying that he doesn't like it by the nonverbal message (head-shaking). Which is the "real" message?

The answer is they're both real, but in conflict. This creates confusion and *completely disrupts synchronized communication*.

One of the key ways you can have problems in communication is by taking all the message channels discussed so far and mixing them up. The messages are *incongruent* when they don't match.

There are two kinds of incongruency, and the first is **Simul-**

taneous **Incongruency** or conflict of verbal and nonverbal messages. That's shaking the head "no" while saying "That's a really nice tie." This is an example of a verbal and nonverbal message in conflict at the same time.

It can also happen with facial expression (message A) and tone of voice (message B). For instance, you walk into a manager's office and he says pleasantly (tone of voice), "Come in, sit down. Good to see you." At the same time, he is looking at you (facial expression) as if the plague (or the IRS) just walked in.

Usually, when you experience incongruency, there's some conflicting information that you don't know the nature of. The way to deal with this is, first, to take in as much information as possible about what's going on. Check the person visually and auditorily. Second, depending on the relationship you have, you can comment on the communication. You might say, "I noticed this morning when I was in your office that you *told* me that you were happy to see me, but you didn't *look* happy. Your tone of voice was pleasant, but by your facial expression, you could have been upset. What was going on?" The manager's explanation might be, "I'm sorry. I was happy to see you, but I've had a bad week, and I didn't get any sleep last night. If I looked like I didn't care about you being there, that's not true. I really did feel okay." This happens all the time! That's why you can't jump to conclusions about what a message "really" means.

The second incongruency pattern is called **Sequential Incongruency**. This happens when your boss has told you for an entire year what a great job you've done. Then at the end of the year, you get a notice of salary increase and your raise is zero. Message A is "good job, good performance." What's the logical Message B? That you'll get a good performance appraisal and a decent raise. However, in this case, Message B does not match the other set of verbal and nonverbal messages you have received over a period of time.

In their study of top executives, McCall and Lombardo (1983) discovered that successful managers intuitively realized the value of clear, congruent communication. They sum this up in their discussion of executive integrity:

"Integrity seems to have a special meaning to executives. The word does not refer to simple honesty, but embodies a consistency and predictability built over time that says, 'I will do exactly what I say I will do, when I say I will do it. If I change my mind, I will tell you well in advance so you will not be harmed by my actions.' Such a statement is partly a matter of ethics, but, even more, a question of vital practicality. This kind of integrity seems to be the core element in keeping a large, amorphous organization from collapsing in its own confusion."

What Makes A Top Executive, pp. 30-31.

Incongruent communication is completely disruptive of supportive, rapport-building behavior. It causes debilitating confusion that interferes with good morale and productive employee relations, and it fosters an environment of mistrust.

Congruent managers are intuitively found to be easy to work with, dynamic, and to always "mean what they say." They follow their own rules. Similarly, congruent organizations are more productive, as they do not issue policy directives which conflict with actual operations or exhibit management behavior which conflicts with the corporation's goals.

Think about these patterns in terms of setting up teams and task forces. Before you actually get people going on the task, you might have them hold an informal group meeting to develop synchronicity. People don't realize that getting together for rituals such as having coffee and donuts or a cigarette break has a purpose, but it does: to develop mutual communication and support.

Exercise 4

While engaged in a conversation, select an aspect of the other person's verbal or nonverbal communication (expression variables) and deliberately:

1. Match (mirror) the communication you've selected.

Note your reaction and his reaction. Take the same expression variable and deliberately;

2. Mismatch.

This exercise develops your ability to successful synchronize communication styles.

Summary

In this chapter, we explored some applications of being able to accurately read communication. Specifically, we covered:

1. Elementary cognitive strategies for enhancing thinking ability;
2. Interpreting and reinforcing negative and positive behavior;
3. Synchronizing communication styles for establishing rapport and influence.

Together, these three sets of patterns form your basic *communication strategies* for developing more productive on-the-job behavior.

The next step is to move beyond simply reading behavior and toward responding to managers and employees in such a way as to better accomplish tasks and goals.

At the end of this chapter, you should be able to recognize communication strategies such as:

- Cognitive strategies which indicate patterns of internal and external preferred sensory modality and rehearsal;
- Interpretation and reinforcement of negative and positive experiences;
- Synchronizing communication style to others by matching (mirroring) information processing preferences and expression variables;
- Patterns of communication that are conflicting/incongruent; both simultaneous and sequential.

Action Plan

Do the exercises in this chapter.

Devote one minute each day to actively mismatching one aspect of someone's communication style such as preferred sensory modality, voice quality, posture, etc. Observe the effect this has on your sense of empathy and rapport.

Pick one work-related experience each week and deliberately express an incongruent message to an individual. Then observe the effect this has upon any decision-making processes between you.

Jockeying For Position

3

Relationships And Personal Influence

In any corporation, employees witness various changes in management and policy and the effects such changes have on their working environment. They often have an indication that a power play is taking place and that influence and control are changing hands. A manager may be mysteriously "reassigned" or promoted to a position of less responsibility. A co-worker may suddenly rise to the top of the corporate ladder for no overt reason.

How are power and influence acquired? Are there underlying "rules of the game" which can tip you off to changes in power? Which you can follow for your own benefit? The answers may lie in understanding the nature of your interpersonal relationships and how they are established and maintained.

The Structure of Relationships

Symmetrical Versus Complementary Relationships

When you put two people together in any situation, what affects their behavior is the *relationship* they have or are establishing.

Dr. Paul Watzlawick (1977) encapsulates the importance of communication and relationships in the following statement:

"It is one of the basic laws of communication that all behavior in the presence of another person has message value, in the sense that it defines and modifies the *relationship** between these people. All behavior says something: for example, total silence or lack of reaction clearly implies, 'I don't want to have anything to do with you.' And since this is so, it's easy to see how much room there is for confusion and conflict."

How Real Is Real?, pp. 6-7.

There are two general types of relationships you can have with anyone, and these definitions are not dependent on culture or ethnic background. The two types of relationships are termed **Symmetrical** and **Complementary**. How you behave at any given time will depend upon whether you *have,* or are *establishing,* a symmetrical or complementary relationship with someone.

Watzlawick, et al., (1967) sums up Gregory Bateson's (1972) ideas of symmetrical and complementary relationships as follows:

"... symmetrical and complementary interaction ... can be described as relationships based on either equality or difference. In the first case the partners tend to mirror each other's behavior, and thus their interaction can be *symmetrical.* Weakness or strength, goodness or badness, are not relevant here, for equality can be maintained in any of these areas. In the second case one partner's behavior complements that of the other, forming a different sort of behavioral Gestalt, and is called *complementary.* Symmetrical interaction, then, is characterized by equality and the minimization of difference, while complementary interaction is based on the maximization of difference.

(*Italics mine—JPE)

There are two different positions in a complementary relationship. One partner occupies what has been variously described as the superior, primary, or 'one-up' position, and the other the correspondingly inferior, secondary, or 'one-down' position. These terms are quite useful as long as they are not equated with 'good' or 'bad,' 'strong' or 'weak.' A complementary relationship may be set by the social or cultural context (as in the cases of mother and infant, doctor and patient, or teacher and student), or it may be the idiosyncratic relationship of a particular dyad. In either case, it is important to emphasize the interlocking nature of the relationship, in which dissimilar but fitted behaviors evoke each other. One partner does not impose a complementary relationship on the other, but rather each behaves in a manner which presupposes, while at the same time providing reasons for, the behavior of the other: the definitions of the relationship fit."

Pragmatics of Human Communication, pp. 68-69.

Thus, in the work environment, a symmetrical relationship is one in which you are on the same level with someone (i.e., peer, co-worker, colleague, or manager/manager, vice-president/vice-president, etc.). A complementary relationship is one in which you have superior/subordinate roles (manager/section head, section head/staff, president/vice-president, etc.).

The type of relationship you have with an employee will determine *how* you communicate with them, whether or not you offend them, and in the long run, can greatly affect your career. Knowing the type of relationship answers the important question, "How do I behave?" with someone and dictates how you can modify your behavior to initiate changes in your organization.

The purposes of categorizing relationships are twofold. First, you can analyze (read) the potential influence of one person over another (including yourself). Second, you can strategize (feed) to establish relationships with employees which can assist you in getting your job done more effectively, or influence others to do the same. This analyzing and strategizing for specific relationships is the "personal touch" in business.

Formal Versus Informal Relationships

Suppose you are a manager at the XYZ Company, and Sam Subordinate is on your sales force. You have a complementary relationship with Sam. Unbeknownst to you, Sam grew up next door to the XYZ Company's president's son and has known Mr. President since he was in diapers. Over the course of time, you decide that Sam is an ineffective and inefficient employee and is doing a lousy job. You start pressing Sam to come up to standards, and when he fails, you try to fire him. But notice how what appears to be a complementary relationship may be reversed on another level of analysis.

Within each symmetrical or complementary relationship, there are two sub-categories which govern the structure of the relationship: *formal* and *informal*.

Formal and informal relationships flip-flop and, thus, can be ambiguous. For example, when you sit in your boss's office, talking and joking about sports and other people, your *informal* relationship is symmetrical. That is, you treat each other as peers within the context of a private conversation. Or take the case of a manager and employee who go out and have lunch together because they've worked for XYZ Company for twenty-five years. They started having lunch together fifteen years ago. Their informal relationship is symmetrical when they go out to lunch. But when they come back to the office, it changes and becomes complementary.

Thus, your friends and acquaintances are your informal relationships which have evolved gradually through exchanges of personal information and thoughts. (Generally, there is also a certain amount of synchronizing or mirroring in informal relationships.)

History (*old* versus *new* information) also plays a part in influencing relationships. Knowing something that others don't know about a program, business deal or individual's personal life can alter the structure of a relationship. Group or organization history is the same. What evolves between two or more people over a long period of time becomes important. They will form a whole complex of communication patterns that subsequently influences power and influence in the corporate decision-making process.

Interpreting Relationships: Rules

Most individuals have rules and limitations as to how close they want to become to another person. How managers and employees jockey for position depends on their rules about relationships and the type of influence they want to establish.

Often, when you get a group of managers together at a company sponsored function, they may behave differently than they do in the symmetrical relationships established at the office. In informal situations, they may establish "one-up/one-down" relationships as a type of "power play."

A lot of employees are more comfortable with not being close to their boss. They prefer to maintain a formal-complementary relationship and resist any informality.

The rules that people have about their relationships are based on how much *Inclusion* or *Exclusion* they desire and are a function of their personal goals concerning power and influence.

The following is a typical pattern. You have a formal relationship with an employee that is complementary. You have another employee who takes the initiative to make your relationship symmetrical, at an informal level, by asking you out to lunch. Your rule might be, "I'm not going to have lunch with my employees except at official functions." Maybe that's an expression of your rules of inclusion and exclusion. Or maybe you're the type that lunches only with certain "underlings."

The idiom that applies here is "playing favorites." Establishing an informal-symmetrical relationship could be viewed as that. How it is interpreted depends upon how subtly you handle it.

You could be upfront with the person about your personal rules. You could say, "It's nothing personal, but I have a rule about having lunch with my employees (which some managers do), and I appreciate your wanting to have lunch with me."

You are learning to move from simple communication patterns to more complex social and political interactions. It is very important to understand the assumptions, presuppositions, and relationships between co-workers in order to execute good, clear communication and to exert your influence to those who can get the job done.

If you are "passed over" for a symmetrical relationship, you need not "take it personally." It is personal in the sense that your communication styles may not match the other person and/or you have not modified your communication style to establish rapport with the other person. You may *consciously or unconsciously* be aware of the fact that you have chosen not to see eye-to-eye, or to click, or to get in touch with a particular person. What will make a difference in whether or not you "get your feelings hurt" or have flexibility about the situation is acknowledging that these patterns are occurring. You might say to yourself, "Now that I think about it, my communication style really doesn't match his, and it would be very difficult for me to change that. I feel that in this situation, it's not worth it to change." That may be a logical decision, especially when you have taken factors about relationships into account.

You probably have also been in the reverse situation, where you become so interested in some person or project that you completely adapt your communication style and patterns to form a relationship with that person or group *and* you have been accepted. Being aware of what your interests, priorities, and goals are will increase your flexibility in forming relationships. This, in turn, increases your ability to influence others for positive work-related outcomes.

Exercise 5

Reproduce the chart on the next page and list in each quadrant two employees you work with and the type of formal and informal relationship you have with them.

	Symmetrical	Complementary
F O R M A L	Betty John	Max Jane
I N F O R M A L	Roscoe Bruno	Susan Richard

After completing the chart, ask yourself:

1. How specifically do I know what my relationship with _____ is? What are the cues that form my determination?

2. Are there any relationships I want to change? What about my communication would I have to change to do this?

This exercise will assist you in reformulating your current business associations in the structural model proposed in this chapter.

Cues For Recognizing Relationships

You use the group of patterns called expression variables or PME's as the cues for identifying the kind of relationships people are trying to establish with you. (These are the individual patterns of verbal and nonverbal communication: tone and tempo of voice, grammatical structures, posture, gestures, spatial rules, etc.)

You may have heard the phrase, "speaking with authority." That's a label that's given to a certain tone of voice and posture. That's an example of a cue as to what kind of relationship a person wants to establish with you. You could interpret it as being intimidating, or a signal of a "one-up/one-down" complementary relationship. It's indicative of *jockeying for position* or determining who is in charge.

One manager I know has a certain authoritarian volume and tone of voice that he has had his whole life. (Maybe his mother or father had those voice qualities.) He's used to hearing it and used to talking that way. *He* doesn't think he's being authoritarian. He doesn't think he's setting up complementary relationships with everyone he works with. But a lot of other employees think of him as a dominant, loud person who's the Napoleon of the office. They interpret his mannerisms as "I'm in control here and we do it my way," and will respond accordingly.

Another postural and spatial rule is about eye level. Here's an example of using an expression variable as a form of cue for establishing relationships. I noticed over the years that I slouched somewhat when I was sitting. I realized that for years, I had unconsciously set up symmetrical eye level with people so that I would be looking at them, however high or low they were sitting (within reason). It was an unconscious way of making eye contact with people and gaining support by establishing a symmetrical relationship.

Grammatical style also influences the type of relationship someone is establishing, and therefore power and action. Verbal communication, like nonverbal communication, may unconsciously influence your behavior. Consider "why questions."

There's a semantic association related to "why" questions. If you ask someone "why" they did something, you also give an embedded message, "*You should (or should not) do behavior X.*" You imply that you don't like some behavior, and the problem is that this is not a direct way to convey that you like or dislike a behavior.

If you ask an employee, "Why were you late?" you're *also* saying, "You shouldn't be late. I don't like it. Why are you doing it?"

What effect does the word "should" have? Think back to your childhood, when your parents told you that you "should" or "shouldn't" do something. Using this word has a tendency to *put people on the defensive.* When someone asks, "Why are you doing that?", the question is interpreted as an accusation, particularly when combined with certain gestures, facial expressions, and tone of voice.

In a simple verbal/grammatical structure such as "why" questions, there are many hidden meanings. When you use them, you can often signal a complementary relationship when you don't mean to, thereby confusing issues of rapport and influence.

If you ask an adult a "why" question, their reaction is often, "Who are you to talk to me this way?" This complex verbal cue often inadvertently generates a kind of "one-up/one-down" reaction.

There are two ways you can ask for personal information. You can either ask somebody a question straight ("Why are you doing this?" "What's going on?") or you can *ask permission to ask.*

In America, this is part of our politeness conventions. It does not confuse the relationship by inadvertently sending a double message. Whenever you are on shaky ground, before actually asking what you want to ask, ask permission to inquire first ("Do you mind if I ask you a question about your relationship with so and so? Do you mind if I ask you a question about what's going on here? Do you mind if I ask you a question about being late"). This is much less accusatory, and *most people will not react defensively to it.*

Let's return to Dr. Max from Chapter 2 and apply these rules. As Dr. Max's patient, you could ask permission to inquire; then ask, "I notice that when you're listening to me, your eyes are closed, and it bothers me. I was wondering if you're aware of that?" First ask if the person is aware of the process. Next, to gather the explanation, you could ask "why" their eyes are closed, but it is better to say, "What does closing your eyes mean to you?" This is preferable to asking "why" as it shows sensitivity and is not accusatory. Asking "What does (x) mean?" or "Do you know what's going on with you when your eyes are closed?" is simpler and less offensive than "*Why* are your eyes closed?"

If your boss comes in to work, and you sense, nonverbally, that something is wrong, you will probably meet defensiveness if you ask, "Why are you in a bad mood today?" But you could say, "I noticed that you look as if something's bothering you. I wanted to know if there is anything going on that I should be aware of. Did the last meeting go poorly?" This approach allows the relationship to remain unambiguous and your ability to influence to remain flexible.

Street Smarts

The consequences of not knowing the principles of informal/formal and symmetrical/complementary relationships can be catastrophic. On the other hand, if you really understand the formal and informal relationships, you're going to get what you want more often. You need to include this information in all your decision-making and prescriptions for action. This is what's called business savvy or *street smarts*.

Sample Case 1: Networking For Promotion And Transfer

The concepts of relationships apply to networking. A good example of networking is transferring from one department to another and perhaps gaining a promotion as well. To illustrate: say you get to know someone outside the department you work in (a manager that can hire you), and you establish an *informal-symmetrical* relationship. Later on, through the networking process, you get hired by that manager, and the *informal-symmetrical* relationship turns into one that is *formal-complementary*.

However, when you change from one department to another, and the business relationship changes, the manager's behavior toward you may also change. Note that when there is a shift in relationships, either formally or informally, the communication clues that accompany the relationship will also change (posture, voice quality, gestures, spatial rules, etc.).

The following outline will help you conceptualize networking, promotion, and transfer in the context of the relationship model presented here.

Your Present Job

Department A
"your boss"

relationship:
formal—complementary
informal—none

Your Future Job

Department B
"new boss"

relationship:
formal—none
informal—none

To transfer:

1. Network by establishing an informal-complementary ("mentor") relationship or informal-symmetrical ("peer") relationship with your potential new boss.
2. Formalize networking by making your goals explicit to your potential new boss and then following proper corporate procedures and etiquette for transferring from one department to another.

A promotion will demand a similar pattern of networking, except that you will move up the hierarchy as you transfer from one department to another.

Thus, a flow chart for networking and obtaining a transfer and/or promotion would look like this:

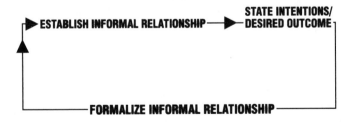

Figure 3

Exercise 6

Max and George meet each other in some unspecified place at some unspecified time. Relying on the sentences below, you are to determine what kinds of possible relationships are expressed. Pay close attention to the differences between the examples, your reactions to them, and how the sentences might affect your analysis.

1. Max: "I'm not myself today."
   George: "Are you feeling all right?"

2. Max: "I'm not myself today."
   George: "Then who are you?"

3. Max: "You know, George, I'm just not myself today."
   George: "Well, then, Max, for the life of me I don't know who you are."

This exercise develops your analytical ability regarding how relationships can be verbally expressed. A simple interaction between two people is packed with valuable information.

If you cannot determine the possible relationships between Max and George in any of the above examples, what other cues would you need?

Summary

This chapter explores how relationships can be analyzed and established. This reveals how so-called political decisions are sometimes made and how you can intentionally form relationships to obtain your work-related outcomes. Specifically covered were:

1. Symmetrical relationships, and;
2. Complementary relationships.

Additionally, we discussed how these two types of relationships can be either formal or informal (or both) and how this can influence the course of action you should take. At the end of this chapter, you should be able to recognize patterns of relationships such as:

• Symmetrical and complementary relationships;
• Formal and informal categories of symmetrical and complementary relationships in your business;
• Patterns of inclusion and exclusion in regard to relationships.

Also, you should be able to form strategies for the type of relationships you want to establish and the ones you want to maintain.

Action Plan

Do the exercises in this chapter.

Devote five minutes each day to observing the interactions of any two people you don't know. Attempt to determine what their relationship is, and then ask yourself, "What communication cues did I notice that influenced my analysis?"

Pick one person with whom you have a close, informal-symmetrical relationship. Now imagine that you become either a subordinate, peer, or superior. Analyze how the formal change would affect your informal relationship. Jot down any changes in communication that might occur between you and the co-worker.

Framing

4

Managing Management Context

The information presented so far is part of a larger context or *frame of reference*. All communication and relationships occur within a context and influence whether your business dealings are successful or not.[1]

As a manager or employee, you know that having some control over the context within which you're operating is extremely important. Whether that context is a sale, negotiation, or salary review, getting a handle on the situation and its outcome is a key factor in achieving your goals. So let's examine the process of framing—an important tool for achieving managerial excellence.

The process of marking or punctuating communication is called *framing*. You put communication in a specific context or frame of reference and assign the communication a contextual meaning.

For example, depending on the business situation, some statements are appropriate or inappropriate. Some actions strike you as humorous or serious. You deem some sequences of communication as appropriate in a specific, mutually agreed upon context and predicate different outcomes and responses from people in that context. There is an entire set of *rules of conduct* or *interaction* that apply to the corporate environment you're in.

An example of a frame is a meeting. Meetings have certain communication patterns which are appropriate and which identify them as meetings as opposed to something like a sale. Within the frame of meetings, there are subframes or subcontexts that determine what kind of meeting it is. It may be a product or program review; a problem-solving meeting; a performance review or appraisal; a termination meeting; a quality circle; a medical diagnosis; a legal briefing, etc. Each of these subcontexts has its own communication patterns which dictate behavior.

A frame, then, is a boundary you place with respect to an event, or series of events, complete with its rules of appropriateness. The first idea to keep in mind is to observe the etiquette (rules) of the frame that you're in for maximum control of your goals/outcomes.

As an employee or manager, there are times when you don't have enough verbal or nonverbal information to determine the most productive behavior for a certain situation. You are liable to make up interpretations that may or may not be correct and may mismark the frame you're operating in. This often leads to unproductive communication habits and the inevitable "faux pas."

Most managers and employees have been in a situation where they were not quite sure what they were expected to contribute and what the goals of the interaction were. This has a disorienting effect and impedes your ability to perform. When context is misread, unproductive, inappropriate behavior can follow. Reading context correctly leads to a smoother problem-solving process in which behavioral norms are understood and goals clearly stated.

The brilliant manager is the one who frames a problem situation correctly. He reads the people correctly, knows (or asks for) the outcomes needed to solve the problem, and gives appropriate feedback to those involved.

Recognizing Frames: Context Cues

A context can be framed verbally or nonverbally, by using spatial rules of communication. An employee's office—and its size and location—is a spatial domain that marks the nature of his relationship to others. Where you say something (space/location) is an important variable in communication. It's a nonverbal communication frame, and in different spatial domains, messages will carry different meanings.

One of the key elements in framing communication is the notion of sequencing—that is, how a segment of communication is sequenced (who initiates an interaction, who terminates it, and how it is initiated and terminated). The sequence of messages indicates what kind of relationship someone has with you or is trying to establish. This information is an important clue to the meaning of a message and the overall meaning of the frame you're operating in.

Here's an example of sequencing of events which may frame communication. Joe Manager, at his desk, wants to give a message to an employee. He can do two things; he can either call the employee into his office or he can go to the employee's office. These interactions can be interpreted very differently, and, depending on the kind of message conveyed, the manager will have to think carefully about framing the interaction. Who initiates communication is important. If you're called into your boss's office, you know that it's marked as something important even though you have a very good informal relationship. This is different from simply walking by, wandering in, or asking how he is today. Initiation of communication projects different frames, and usually marks the communication and relationship as complementary or symmetrical.

Preferred Sensory Modality (PSM) also indicates the behavior and goals of a specific frame. For example, the media of a context may be visual, auditory or kinesthetic and will accordingly dictate what is expected. A marketing review of a new product may require elaborate visual presentations such as brochures, films, view graphs, slides, etc., and form an integral part of the context (frame). An international negotiation may require auditory communication in the form of clandestine discussions. Or a government proposal may require a certain type of written response accompanied by an actual "walk through" or "fly off" of the product. All these sensory-oriented components of communication help to form the boundaries of the context/frame you're operating in. They are your guidelines and tools for managing people and situations.

Certain types of verbal communication also provide cues for interpreting frames. In *The Structure of Magic, Vol. I* (1975), John Grinder and Richard Bandler introduce the idea of *nominalizations*—a complex process which becomes conceptualized as a *thing* or event. For example, the process of *leading* becomes relabeled as *leadership* and the intricacies of the process are overlooked when they become discussed as a "thing" and not a process.

Nominalizations provide a verbal clue for recognizing frames and thus identifying the intricacies and underlying rules of the meaning of context. The key lies in identifying a frame, usually verbally indicated by a nominalization, and asking yourself the following:

1. What are my goals and assumptions with respect to [insert nominalization/frame]?
2. What is/are my relationship(s) with respect to the individuals involved in [insert nominalization/frame]?
3. What are the various rules of communication and communication styles of the individuals involved in [insert nominalization/frame]?

Consider *leadership*. You may ask yourself: what are my assumptions about good, effective leadership? What are my goals? How would I know if I was a good leader? A bad one? What is my present relationship to those around me and how does that affect my ability to lead others? How does my communication style affect those around me? Is it the most desirable for leading my department? My company?

Take a look at the list of nominalizations in Exercise 7. These are in effect frames of reference you need to analyze for influencing communications, relationships, goals and assumptions.

Exercise 7

The following is a list of some common business frames (represented by nominalizations). Pick five of them and list three rules that define the boundaries or limits of the frame.

Meeting	Manufacturing
Delegating	Sales/Marketing
Performance	Research and
Evaluation	Development (Design)
Productivity	Distribution
Management	Negotiation

An easy way to approach this is to ask yourself, "What would have to happen (or not happen) for the frame to be defined?"

Note that some frames, for their definition, are more dependent on location than others (manufacturing and meetings). Some are more dependent on specific interactions of people (delegation), and others on things such as money (sales).

This exercise develops your ability to define contexts and ascribe meaning to a particular context. Think about how you use your overall communication style (PSM, PTS, expression variables) to punctuate frames of reference and to give a context a certain meaning.

Sample Case 1: Terminating Conversations

Every relationship has politeness conventions that frame its interaction. One of the most delicate areas is that of terminating conversations. A manager might stand up and start toward the door and most likely an employee will take this as a nonverbal frame (punctuation) that the conversation has ended. Another nonverbal frame would be glancing at your watch. You can give a lot of nonverbal signals that aren't rude. A verbal frame might be to say, "I have some reports I have to prepare for a meeting. Thanks for coming by."

Breaking people off from a conversation is sometimes difficult because they do not follow the rules of the frame. For some people, you practically have to say, "Excuse me, but the conversation is ending." If you have to do this (comment overtly on the interaction), it might signal that unclear communication had occurred.

Sometimes people are oblivious to the fact that you're glancing at your watch, or that you're working on some project at your desk, or that you're right in the middle of an assignment. It's not that they are rude; they just don't pay attention to what they *see*. You might have to confront them verbally (auditorily) and initiate a verbal frame: "I really enjoy talking with you, but I feel pressured about what I'm doing. Could we continue this later?" That's something auditory people should understand! (These patterns apply to telephone communication as well.)

This is part of your time management. You can lose several hours a week of productive work time due to ill-executed frames such as conversations.

Frames And Systems: Managing Your Goals

A frame is a system with certain characteristics, one of which is stability or *homeostasis*. In any system of interaction, an important characteristic of the system is its ability to remain stable to a certain extent.

An example of a system and stability is a thermostat. You set it at a certain level, and if the room temperature goes above or below that specified limit, the air conditioning or heat kicks on. The room temperature is stabilized around a parameter that's defined by the user and relies on *feedback* for maintaining stability.

In human communication, what indicates stability and defines a system are the explicit goals and the underlying assumptions[2] that you make with respect to the frame you're in. Thus, stability will depend on the goals and assumptions that you have formed within a specific frame of reference (the *parameters*) and whether they have been successfully achieved or not. As an employee, you rely on *feedback* to know if the parameters are secure (if the goals and assumptions are achieved).

When you begin to define your goals and assumptions explicitly, you discover that these are specific to individuals and organizations. What makes *you* satisfied at work won't necessarily make a fellow employee satisfied. And there are various *levels* of goals—company goals, personal goals, and some more or less universal corporate goals such as profit and quality.

From this point of view, what happens to the frame (context) if goals are not reached? This often has a destabilizing effect on people and organizations. Thus, the governing variable in a given frame is the goals and outcomes you want to achieve. This gives a context its meaning to a great extent.

In human terms, goals appear in many guises. A goal may be a "point," an "idea," the "purpose" of something, etc. A goal may have to do with money, power, job-related tasks, acceptance of a policy statement, etc. If goals and assumptions do not remain somewhat stable, confusion and disorientation follow, and your work-related performance can be affected. Suppose you were to walk into an important marketing meeting, which you had prepared for, only to find out that the meeting was now focused on manufacturing costs. You may not be prepared for such a change in the goals of the meeting. You may be angry that you were not informed or you may not be concerned at all.

When goals change, the meaning of the context can shift. Thus, the interpretation of the frame is in question and so is knowing your most practical problem-solving behavior. Managing your goals is a crucial step in exercising some control over the context/frame and successfully managing the business context you're operating in.

The magic of managing context is that you can anticipate problems by being able to predict instability and then orchestrate change.

Organizational Incongruencies

In Chapter 2, you learned about incongruencies or "double messages." They can happen in interactions between individuals or organizations. You may have been in a situation where there are conflicting management decisions about what to do on a certain project and ended up asking yourself, "Who do I believe?" That is evidence of an organizational incongruency or managerial double message.

A common example of double messages is when a corporate policy statement is issued which clearly does not reflect the actual behavior of management. For example, a company may support employee development through the tool of educational reimbursement programs for employee education. However, when the employee goes to receive reimbursement money, he encounters "foot-dragging," questions about his motives, or is told the "kitty" is empty.

In this example, the organizational double message is the goal of employee improvement versus the goal of cost savings. These incongruencies lead to lower morale, increased turnover, and employees who question the integrity of the management.

Anticipating such potentially conflicting frames reflects excellent, pro-active management and fosters a climate of good morale and productivity.

Sample Case 2: The Performance Review

If something is "wrong" in your organization or an interaction that you have with someone else, there is a goal and/or assumption that is not being met.

Let's say you have been given an excellent performance appraisal. You *expect* (assumption) and financially *need* (goal) a good raise. You think you deserve a raise because you have worked hard and received an excellent performance appraisal.

All your interactions and systems of communication have been defined, over time, in terms of your on-the-job performance. You have intuitively realized that there are patterns of communication that you can use to perform well and to get a raise. You also know there are patterns of communication and behavior that may be negative in relation to your work. You (should) know the differences between these patterns.

In this case, you have a goal that you have been working for and an assumption that it's going to occur. This interaction can be called the "performance frame."

Let's say salary review time arrives and you receive a company salary slip that indicates zero dollars. What is your response? Perhaps anger—you've been deceived. There's something wrong with the interaction over time (an incongruency). Think about this sequence of events in terms of *destabilizing* communication. You have built up a pattern of communicating and behaving that depends upon specific goals and assumptions being met—*they give your job and work meaning.* In this case, the goal/assumption is a raise, and when you don't get it, all the assumptions you made in regard to how you communicate, how you feel, how you interact with employees, tasks that you performed at work, etc., are void. You have had the rug pulled out from underneath you and much of what you've done appears "meaning-less" to you.

As a manager and an employee, there should be no destabilizing surprises if good, congruent communication is occurring. Let's say you get a raise, and even if it wasn't what you had hoped for, to a certain degree you should have known (ideally) what you were going to get. That would indicate that the communication between you and your boss was good.

You need to know where *you* stand as an indication of whether good communication has occurred or not. *The measure of this is the degree to which not meeting goals has a destabilizing effect on your people and your organization.*

Exercise 8

Take 15 minutes to focus on your job and the tasks you perform each week. Now list five goals and five assumptions you have with respect to your job.

1. Describe as best you can your individual communication patterns for achieving those goals and assumptions;
2. Think about how you would react if any of your goals and assumptions were suddenly not achieved.

This exercise demonstrates the parameters related to your job which may be destabilizing and thus necessitate change and/or added attention.

Leading Versus Managing: Changing Frames

No set of messages occurs at only one level of interaction or interpretation. An example of levels of messages is formal versus informal relationships. When you think about your relationships, you don't just think about them in terms of simply the formal relationship that's indicated on a corporate organizational chart or simply the informal relationship that you have with a peer or superior. You intuitively think about relationships occurring at more than one level. This same intuition about patterns is true of frames.

When you think about problems at work, you need to think in terms of more than one level, or you're going to inaccurately analyze and respond to a problem situation, and apply inaccurate problem-solving techniques that make the problem worse.

If you have ever led a meeting, you know that the typical behavior to get everyone's attention is to say (auditory), "Can I have your attention, please?" You'll notice that when you give a verbal command, usually about half the people don't pay attention to you. You could give a visual signal in addition to the auditory one (i.e., some kind of hand motion). Shifting the parameters of the frame, that is, intentionally altering your gestures, sensory output and language, can positively influence the outcome of the situation. This indicates that you have analyzed a context at more than one level of interaction and thus increased your behavioral responses.

In a heated courtroom battle or session of Congress, when the judge or speaking is banging the gavel, everyone continues talking. The message is going in *one* channel (auditory). Continuing to beat the gavel indicates responding to only one level or aspect of the problem. If the judge had a light that flashed on and off in the middle of the room, that would probably get the attention of the visual people. Kinesthetically-oriented people would probably need a chair that emitted slight electric shocks!

A leader is one who asks, "What *kind* of problem do we have? Is it centered around miscommunication? Sensory preferences? Thinking style conflicts? A conflict of goals or assumptions?" Leaders are willing to change context by altering the elements of a frame. They are frame-changers as opposed to frame-managers. Leaders recognize shifting goals, assumptions, relationships, and communication and take risks in altering a frame's parameters beyond the status quo.

A leader exhibits flexibility of behavior so that complex business problems can be solved. Addressing this issue, Richard Bandler and John Grinder state (quoted in Daniel Goleman's 1979 article):

"The professional uses feedback to understand the other person's response, and has the flexibility to vary his own behavior until he gets the desired response. There's a principle in cybernetics called the Law of Requisite Variety that demonstrates this mathematically. Take any connected system, whether in electronics or with people, and the element with the widest range of variability in its behavior will always be in control; it will always have that one more response that can make a difference.

Typically, the most successful person in any field is flexible enough to shift to various strategies as the demands change. That's why it's terribly important to teach a kid not just how to get along with people in his own family, but with other people, too. Every family has its channels of acceptable behavior, how to get what you want, and so on. But the set of strategies people learn are different in each family. If you know only the strategies of your family, you'll find they won't work for many things outside of it.

As soon as there are behaviors you can't generate, then there are responses you can't elicit. Children have to learn to vary their behavior in different contexts. The most successful people always know how to vary their behavior, regardless of the rules of the game. The counterpart of this in business is the Peter Principle, that people are promoted past their level of competence. The strategies that will make a person a success at a lower level can make him inflexible or inept at a higher one."

People Who Read People, p. 30.

Have you had a manager you would call really flexible, able to take care of all different kinds of organizational, technical, and people problems? This has a positive effect on the whole department and changes the entire work environment.

All managers are role models for their employees, whether they like it or not. As a role model, if you are flexible and take risks, the employees around you will adopt that behavior to a certain degree and become more flexible and risk-taking (frame-changing) themselves. The net result is the encouragement and of leadership behaviors which are crucial to the success of any corporation.

Decision Criteria For Changing Frames

The following are simple criteria for deciding to enact frame-changing or leadership behaviors (when you are intentionally going to shift the goals, communication, and relationships of the frame you're operating in—"changing the rules of the game").

When the goals and assumptions within a defined frame are not successfully achieved, then change the components of the frame, or, if necessary, change the frame entirely.

Let's look at an example of the involvement of two frames which can lead to the greatest potential for conflict.

Manufacturing And Engineering

Most executives don't think of engineering (design) and manufacturing (production) as two completely different frames which are also completely interdependent. In this case, you can have conflict between frames of reference which may involve changing frames to reach a solution. You may know that there are conflicts between manufacturing and engineering organizations in many ways. Now, let's examine the differences between manufacturing and engineering in terms of frames of reference and patterns of communication.

What is the basic function of engineering in a *pattern* or *process* sense? To design and develop a product. In the process of designing and developing a product, you create a *visual* representation of something; a blueprint. Whether the goal is a space telescope, an automobile, a computer, or a shirt, you're still creating and designing visual representations *of* something *for* something.

What does manufacturing do in a process sense? *Fabricate.* They take visual representations and kinesthetically turn them into physical objects (go from a visual frame to a kinesthetic frame). You have to properly translate from one frame to another (indicating that you understand the rules of translation), or else you generate work-related problems.

In this case, you must decide whether the goals of the *design* frame are more or less important than the goals of the *production* frame. The primary goal of the design frame may be technological advancement over cost. The primary goal of the production frame may be quality and low cost over technological advancement. The larger frame you are operating in (your corporate goals, the marketplace, etc.) will assist you in the decision process. The leader will be aware of this and obtain the information necessary to set priorities for the goals of each frame and put the decision into action.

A lot of conflicts are based on differences in frames of reference and thus require changing aspects of the frame/context. Engineering and manufacturing are examples of this. If you know what rules of behavior differentiate the two, you can use a variety of techniques to reduce the conflict and increase productivity. You often see a lot of effort go into getting conflicting organizations to work together. But at a communication level, few people have an understanding of the differences between the two frames of reference that may require different patterns of thinking and a different kind of problem-solving and solution implementation.

Summary: The Model Up To Now

Up to this point, you have been given pieces of a model of communication that you can use to make the message clear. In Chapter 1, you learned about communication style and the components which make up communication. In Chapter 2, you learned communication strategies you can use to analyze and change behavior. Chapter 3 covered how communication style and strategies are combined in the development of relationships with others. In this chapter, the model was completed by adding goals/outcomes as a factor which influences the direction of your behaviors. This created a tool for interpreting and altering contexts for increased management effectiveness.

All the aspects of communication presented so far do not operate in isolation. They are interconnected and mutually influential. However, there is a hierarchy of influence or feedback in which one aspect of communication has more influence than another (See Figure 4 below).

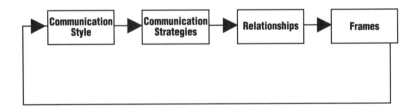

Figure 4

The arrows indicate which aspect of communication "governs" the others, or is inclusive of the other aspects. Thus your relationships consist of your communication style and strategies and your relationships dictate what your communication style and strategies will be.

The next three chapters are primarily applications of the tools presented in the first four chapters, and each deals with specific frames of reference and demonstrates putting the communication tools into action for increased productivity and problem-solving. Specifically, the chapter on criticizing and motivation is concerned with maintaining and enhancing existing frames of reference. The chapter on relabeling and reframing is concerned with changing frames of reference and the components which make up the frames. Finally, the chapter on negotiation is about integrating different frames of reference for obtaining mutually beneficial outcomes.

Enhancing, changing and integrating—these are the key concepts for making the message clear.

At the end of this chapter, you should be able to recognize how communication is given meaning contextually by:

- Defining the frame of reference you are communicating in, as well as the subframe(s);
- Defining the goals and assumptions you have established within a system which stabilizes the system.

Action Plan

Do the exercises in this chapter.

Devote five minutes each day to observing how someone who works with you solves a particular problem. Then ask yourself, "How would I have solved the problem differently? Would I have selected a different behavior as the 'real' problem? If so, what?"

Pick one pattern of behavior/communication each week and (1) deliberately interrupt the pattern, and (2) note your reaction to the interruption. This could be something as simple as skipping or delaying your morning coffee, making phone calls you normally make in the morning in the afternoon, or talking for two minutes with a fellow employee whom you normally go out of your way to avoid.

Getting Employees To Do Things With Words

5

Criticizing And Motivating

Let's shift back to individual behavior as opposed to group behavior and elaborate on some of the verbal skills presented thus far so that you can "get employees to do things with words."

This chapter will deal with motivation and criticism (both are frames in the sense discussed in Chapter 4). They are complex behaviors that involve your knowledge about communication, relationships, and the parameters you set with respect to goals, assumptions, and work-related outcomes.

Criticizing

Employees often relate that they will work hard on a particular project, often with little or no feedback, and when they present their report, design, mock-up, or breadboard phase product, BANG! out of left field comes an inappropriate and unproductive criticism.

Criticism seems to be one of the most fundamental experiences of the working (or schooling) class. Many people have experienced what could be called constructive or positive criticism that either gets you or keeps you on the right track without destroying your self-esteem. On the other hand, you may have suffered the opposite problem—a complete lack of criticism to the point where you are not sure what is expected of you or what your task should be.

There are two senses of the word criticism: punitive, hostile remarks; and constructive and optimally instructive remarks that are not hostile.

Consider your response to the following scenario. An employee, Max, has just finished an important design of a new product that may make a substantial profit for his company. His boss says, "You know, this isn't really what I wanted. Didn't you follow my ideas of what I wanted? And besides, there's a small design error on the corner here. Well, it doesn't matter at this point. Max, I need you to do better."

Now consider how Max might feel if he heard this: "Very good and creative, Max. I see you've put a lot of effort into this new design. I've been doing some thinking, though, and I think we need to sit down and talk about some changes I'd like to make, bounce some ideas off you and see what you think. You have a good concept here, and I think between us we can refine it to include the specific changes I believe our customers will want."

At one time or another, it's likely that you have been subject to both *patterns* of criticism, and the word "pattern" is used deliberately. The differences in these two examples are systematic and learnable. There are ways you can learn to get better criticism and ways to give criticism that are positive, congruent, and productive to you and your employees.

As a manager, you know that effective criticism is important in getting your department to run smoothly and productively. It's also one of the most difficult behaviors to master. As a result, many managers simply don't give criticism or feedback of any type, except if the corporation they work for has a mandatory employee "performance evaluation." Unfortunately, these are usually a yearly or semi-yearly event—hardly enough feedback to create a fully functioning employee or staff. And by the time the performance review comes around (usually around raise time), the manager is so reluctant to give criticism, or has had so little practice giving it, that he does not provide the feedback needed for optimum performance. Most employees live in a performance vacuum, a "twilight zone" of criticism where, after thirty years with a company, they have no idea about their efficacy.

This is not entirely the fault of management. Most of us are not taught how to get good feedback and criticism from those around us, whether it is teachers, parents, co-workers, or supervisors. You need to take the responsibility on yourself to learn what you need, what your patterns are, how to be *positively self-critical*, and how to model this for others.

Learning to be an effective critic of performance assumes a familiarity with the principles of communication you have learned so far. You need to be sensitive and aware of others' communication, and to know what their rules and intentions are or be willing to learn them. Synchronizing for empathy and trust is also exceedingly important for giving good criticism. If employees know they are about to be criticized, they may be especially defensive or closed-off. So you need to be especially aware and to match behavior to the point of maximum comfort.

When management changes in a corporation, it is difficult both for the new manager to give accurate criticism to the employees and for the employees to take criticism from new management seriously. There is a "credibility gap" which is really a "knowledge gap." Giving criticism in such an environment is confusing at best. From a strategic point of view, a corporation should hold off on management changes if possible until right after yearly performance reviews so that the new supervisor has a chance to get to know everybody and develop a shared knowledge base.

Let's take a look at Roscoe, Max's supervisor. He needs to create the most effective critique of Max's work. The first consideration of the criticism model is that of developing a *shared knowledge base*. It's difficult to give in-depth and meaningful criticism without common knowledge of what is expected of the employee, knowledge of exactly what the employee does, and the importance of his tasks in the larger context of the company.

Max is in his boss's office for his yearly performance review. His supervisor, Roscoe, has greeted Max at his office door, asked him to sit at a side table away from his main desk, and told him to make himself comfortable. Roscoe engages Max in some brief small talk, roughly adopting Max's posture, gestures, facial expression, etc. Most importantly, Roscoe has reviewed both Max's formal job description, the specific tasks Max has been recently working on, and his progress on them. Finally, Roscoe has networked with other employees to see if Max has had any pressing personal/medical problems that may be affecting his work.

Max is a software engineer for the Kiddyware software company and is currently working on a new math game for elementary school children that is supposed to help them learn arithmetic. He recently got married to his long-time girlfriend and is in post-marital bliss. Now that Roscoe has established his shared knowledge base, he can proceed to the task at hand.

The second important aspect of criticism that Roscoe needs to consider is the *sequence* of messages in the criticism. For best effect in making the criticism instructive and productive, he needs to *sequence* his communication as follows: complimentary/instructive message; corrective/instructive message; complimentary/instructive message. Roscoe should start with something that is complimentary and instructive in nature so that the following messages can be more clearly heard and enacted. To start out with a negative message, even a corrective one, may put Max on the defensive. Even if Roscoe thinks Max is a bad employee, to start with, "Max, I'm disappointed in your work. You're five minutes from being fired" probably won't help him to establish a close, meaningful sense of rapport and empathy with Max.

The third component of effective criticism has to do with how *specific* you are. You may have had the experience of getting vague task directions followed by even more vague, more convoluted criticism. It puts you in a "no-win" situation since it's hard to defend yourself or know which direction to go when the information you receive is as elusive as (as the writer Brautigan put it) "shoveling mercury with a pitchfork." Phrases like "sort of," "this isn't really what I meant," "not really," "kind of," and "do it all over and bring it back to me" do not make for good criticism and may only result in raising someone's blood pressure.

The last aspect of criticism is an important and essential one—*criticize the task, not the person.* This may or may not seem obvious, but it is difficult to do without practice and very damaging to morale and productivity if not followed. A common scenario, with disastrous results, is when a manager "mixes intentions," starts out critiquing an employee's work and ends up making personally critical, hostile comments. If you're having problems with an employee, such as behavior or discipline problems, this should optimally be made clear to him beforehand.

Connected to the idea of criticizing the task is the ability to be *corrective* and *goal-oriented* in your remarks. Ideally, you want to be able to say exactly *what* you need the worker to do differently or better and also to tell him what he is already doing well so that he can keep doing it.

Sample Case 1: Criticizing For Results

Let's look at some contrasting examples. Roscoe is sitting with Max and is about to give him his semi-annual performance evaluation.

Message 1

"Well, Max, I understand that you're progressing right on schedule with the new Kiddyware math game for six to nine year olds. In all honesty, that's unusual in this business! Creating good quality software is a tough job for anyone."

Message 2

"Some of the staff and I have recently been looking over some of our competitor's bestselling software, and I think we might want to alter some of the graphics in your package. What I want to do after our meeting today is get together with a couple of other staff members to go over the other software products and to see what you think. I know with your capabilities that you'll be able to continue producing outstanding software."

Message 3

"Max, looking over your work, I see that your sequencing of material is pedagogically excellent. I've also gotten some of this feedback from some of the teacher/user groups we've contacted.

I'm thinking that perhaps you could get together with some of our instructional writers and come up with some guidelines for newer members of our staff who need some help in this area."

In Message 1, you can see that the initial positive message specifically addresses the task that Max is currently working on for Kiddyware. Message 2 is also specific as far as the task Max's boss thinks should be corrected. Roscoe doesn't say exactly *what* to do, but *how* to go about it in a goal-oriented way as opposed to a personal/evaluative way. Message 3 ends on a positive note and is also task-oriented; it shows a direction Roscoe would like Max to follow.

You can get an even better sense of the value of this pattern of criticism by contrasting it with another set of messages from Roscoe's alter-ego. Keep in mind that your intuitions about good, productive communication and bad, unproductive communication are based on the kind of verbal and nonverbal components covered so far—and that these patterns are learnable for improved business communication.

Message 1A
"Well, Max, I understand the graphics on that program you're working on haven't been as good as our competitor's. Is this job too much for you? Or perhaps you're not familiar with our needs on this project."

Message 2A
"I hear you're pretty good at sequencing material so that our users like it. You must have had some good instruction in that area or been at this game for a long time."

Message 3A
"Max, get on that graphics program, will you, or I mean, on improving the graphics. Perhaps you can work on it with, ah, George. He has more experience than you with these types of problems."

You might have noticed that these examples reverse everything you learned to do for ideal criticism. They may seem a little far-fetched, but for some employees and managers, this kind of communication represents a "good day."

This set of examples follows an uncomplimentary, complimentary, then uncomplimentary structure. Roscoe's remarks are more personal in nature, not goal-oriented or instructive, and indirectly question Max's ability. They are vague on two levels— they show little evidence of shared knowledge *and* they do not specify aspects of the task that should be improved or what Max is already doing correctly. These examples give Max little sense of what he is doing right or wrong and what goals he is expected to achieve. Max is in the "twilight zone" of criticism. His next move may be to send out several resumes.

Crazy-Making

What happens in all too many companies is the following. You are given the barest of guidelines for a particular project (perhaps simply the topic for a report and its approximate length). Your first mistake is to begin the task at that point, with little feedback. But let's say you work hard for two weeks putting together a financial report or design review and then turn it in. You are not only negatively criticized for the report, but *you're criticized for not doing a task you were not specifically asked to do. AND you're criticized for doing tasks that you were told would be inappropriate!* Such behavior is all too common and can result in "feeling crazy" when you are on the receiving end.

Criticism As A Frame Of Reference

Criticism is a *frame of reference* for employees. It punctuates an employee's behavior and communication by specifying the goals and tasks the employee needs to know in order to answer the question (frame) "what's going right?" and "what's going wrong that needs to be corrected?" It *enhances* an employee's ongoing performance by providing a powerful formula for feedback.

As mentioned earlier, ideal criticism is instructive in its

outcome and removes employees from the "twilight zone" of criticism. It is achieved by the following steps:

1. Establish a shared knowledge base between manager and employee;
2. Sequence your messages as follows: complimentary/instructive; corrective/instructive; complimentary/instructive;
3. Be specific in your criticism—avoid words such as *it, this, that, these, those, things,* etc., unless there is a common understanding of what they refer to. Avoid hedges such as *sort of, kind of,* etc.;
4. Criticize the task, not the person.

In the long run, if tasks are not spelled out specifically and corrective instruction is not given, the frame will be incomplete for you and your employee and may result in destabilizing, unproductive behavior.

Exercise 9

Take the time to think of two employees you know in your company, one you know well and one not so well. Conceptualize a criticism of their performance following the guidelines on pages 71-78. They are:

1. Shared knowledge;
2. Sequencing of messages;
3. Specificity of message;
4. Criticizing task, not person.

Now write a brief evaluation based on the criteria above. Compare and contrast the level of difficulty for writing about the person you know well versus the one you know less well. What were the differences? What do you need to know or do to make the evaluation/criticism process more equitable? Easier for yourself? This exercise helps you to conceptualize how to criticize employees in terms of the model set forth in this chapter.

Success and Failure: Motivating Employees

Motivation is an issue you may have faced in a management situation. The model presented in this section will show you how to get people to do things (motivate them) with words. First, think about the *difference* between criticism and motivation. Most employees, managers, and companies confuse the two all the time and end up both ineffective and frustrated. They say, "Well, we tried that and it didn't work. We spent all that money and no one did anything better or differently. What a waste. We'll just have to go back to the old ways; at least we know what we're up against."

Such scenarios are all too common in corporations and with individual managers. But successful companies and managers know, at least intuitively, the difference between criticism and motivation.

Criticism, as defined previously, involves assessing and evaluation an employee's *tasks* and *goals*. Motivation involves assessing something much more complex—how individual employees *think about themselves* on the job.

One of the cardinal sins of mismanagement—one that is committed all too frequently and can cause low morale and inefficiency—is trying to motivate people *before* they have a mutually agreed upon set of work-related goals and tasks with their management. Employees need to know who or what they're cheering for *before* they go to the game.

Let's take a look at *patterns* of motivating people and organizations. Often, the thoughts that individuals have and use to evaluate their work experience are made *in relation to their personal ideas about their own success and failure on the job*. In other words, without understanding what constitutes success or failure for Max, you're going to have a difficult time motivating Max.

At one time, you may have asked yourself, "What's important to me at this job? How does working here affect my career? How does it fit in with my long- and short-term goals in my personal, present and/or future family life? How will I know when I'm successful at this job? At this company? How will I know when I've failed?" Those managers and employees who have not asked and answered these questions for themselves are the most dissatisfied and the most difficult to motivate.

Another way of putting it is this: how do you measure success? Money? Power? Intellectual stimulation? Management challenges? Office space? How many friends you've made? How famous you've become? Flexible working hours? Or some combination of the above? Each person has his own "success formula" that is measured by the number of success and failure criteria obtained. When an employee's criteria are not met, unmotivated, low-productivity behavior will often occur. *How you think about yourself, your job, etc. is made in relation to having achieved these criteria.*

Rewards, Reprimands, Praise, Punishments, Seductions, And Incentives

Say you are a supervisor. You've given Max a big raise, and his performance hasn't improved. You threw big office parties, and it didn't seem to make a difference. You moved Maxine into a smaller office and she doesn't seem to be getting the message. You promoted a supervisor to the level of manager, and they still complain about the same old lack of challenges. And on and on. The lesson of these scenarios is that you have failed to assess employees' ideas of personal success and failure. A reprimand or a reward is only as good as the linkage between it and the employee's idea of success or failure.

Motivation, like criticism, is a frame of reference. It's a complicated piece of behavior that involves personal goals and outcomes. It can be used to enhance employee performance. As a manager, you may have the best of intentions in trying to "get so and so off the dime" or "give so and so that pat on the back" you think they need. But in the process, you're not aware of their own success-related goals. Confusing, unproductive behavior may occur—just after you thought you really motivated someone.

"Getting Max Off The Dime": Attributing Causes To Successes And Failures[1]

Motivation involves either getting someone to do more of a good thing or getting someone to do a good thing that they're not doing well enough. We've started to examine a model that you can use, like criticism, to get people to do things with words.

Let's say Max didn't get the raise he thought he deserved, and he feels badly about it. He's puzzled and at the same time is having a multitude of kinesthetic, gut-level reactions—anger, shame, fear. He has worked like a dog and come up empty-handed. The typical reaction to this is to *try to attribute a cause or causes to his perceived failure* or lack of goal achievement. He has, in a manner of speaking, a broken frame, and may wonder, "Was it something I did? Something I didn't do? Maybe it wasn't me at all—after all, this new boss is a jerk. Well, it doesn't matter what I do around here, I always come up with the short end of the stick." At this time, Max may not be too motivated. He may "get mean" and try twice as hard. But we already have one clue—he measures success in part by money. This is an important piece of the motivation puzzle.

The causes given here that individuals attribute their success and/or failures to are among the most common and are the most useful to understand.

Usually, employees will attribute their success or failure on the job to either the *ability* or to their *effort* or some combination thereof. This assumes, however, that they are considering the cause to be *internal* to the frame of reference that they are operating in.

Assuming Max thinks he didn't get the raise he thought he deserved because of his own shortcomings, he'll go on a "causal search." He may think, "I must not have tried hard enough" (effort) or "Maybe I don't have what it takes" (ability) or "I must be doing something wrong" (ambiguous feelings about ability or effort).

To get Max "off the dime," the first step is to establish mutually agreed upon work-related tasks. In other words, if Max is a software engineer for Kiddyware, you want to have a good idea of what he does. The *next step,* a critical one, is to assess his personal ideas of success and failure. You may indeed discover that many employees never think about their success and failure. If that's the case, then you'll need to find that out and encourage them to think about it. But assuming that they have some idea of how success is measured for them, then assess what those goals are. *Third,* you'll need to *link* their work-related tasks to their personal notions of success. Otherwise, whatever rewards, incentives, or disciplinary actions you might take will probably fall flat. *Finally,* you'll need to take into account the attributions they'll make about their own work, whether they think they're succeeding or failing due to ability, effort, or "outside forces."

Sample Case 2: Motivating Max

We know what Max does at Kiddyware; we know that getting a good raise signals to Max in his own "frame" that he is doing well. Knowing this, it's possible to *link* the reward of a raise (or the discipline of no raise) to Max's performance on his work-related tasks. Finally, we'll assess Max's ability and his on-the-job effort and sequence a verbal response that will reinforce Max's attributions about his possible success and failure. One scenario might go like this:

Message 1

"Max, you have just about the most *ability* of any of our software engineers at Kiddyware. As a matter of fact, I'd venture to say that you have potentially the most *ability.* But I need you to direct a little more of your *efforts* toward the graphics area of the current software you're working on. We need improvements in that area. I think that if we can turn the graphics around on this program you're working on now, and if the sales reflect that improvement, and I have no doubt that they will, then you'll find that reflected substantially in your raise and bonus this year."

In this example, we see that Max's supervisor has a good idea of what Max does and how Max measures success. His supervisor also links Max's measure of success (money) to his tasks at

Kiddyware. Finally, he takes into account personal attributions of ability and effort when couching his motivating message to Max.

The overall sequence of a motivational message is less crucial than that of criticism. What is more important is the *linking of task and idea of success* and the *sequencing of ability and effort messages* according to your assessment of the employee. In general, if you have assessed an employee's ability and effort and decided that they have the ability for the tasks at hand ("I have no doubt that you can do the job"), then ability messages precede effort messages. If the employee is of marginal ability, then emphasize effort in your messages in lieu of ability. Of course, if the employee's ability does not match the tasks at all, it's time for you to realign the employee with a different, more appropriate set of tasks.

Suppose you are in a situation where you misread an employee's personal ideas of success and failure. You think that for your employee, George, "money talks" like it does for Max. However, George likes his job so much that he almost feels "lucky" to be getting paid to do work he considers an intrinsically challenging task that he would probably do on his own. Much to your astonishment, George has not done what you told him to do after his big raise last year. But you assume that money will talk once again. George, however, likes to be told that he is exceptionally intelligent, superb at what he does. That is, he likes a lot of positive ability attributions. What motivates him is assigning him new and more challenging tasks. Here, he rises to the challenge. So let's look at this example of motivation where George's manager doesn't know how success is measured for this employee.

Message 2
"George, I'm *disappointed with your output* over the past six months. You know, after the big raise you got last year, your performance has not increased significantly. I think *you need to try much harder* than you have been—put out more *effort*. If things don't improve, I may have to *give you less challenging* assignments."

At this point, George is ready to walk. Everything that he needs to be a well-motivated and productive employee has been violated. As a result, George experiences that his boss is insensitive and unaware of his personal goals, abilities, and value as an employee. He becomes despondent, disillusioned, and unproductive. Then he quits and starts a competing firm that becomes Kiddyware's biggest competitor!

The important idea to keep in mind when motivating employees is the employees themselves and their goals and desires. A message to an employee in and of itself may not be "good" or "bad" but rather inappropriate for that particular employee. In sum, good motivation involves:

1. Establishing work-related tasks between employee and supervisor;
2. Assessing an employee's personal ideas of success and failure;
3. Linking an employee's ideas of success and failure to their work-related tasks;
4. Assessing an employee's ability and effort and then taking into account his attributions about his own ability and effort when trying to motivate him.

Exercise 10

As with Exercise 9 in this chapter, pick someone you know well from work and someone you know less well. Repeat the exercise, this time conceptualizing a motivating message according to the criteria listed above. Note the differences.

A Note On "Outside Forces"

Many times, factors outside of a particular frame of reference influence what goes on within another frame. As mentioned in Chapter 4, there are levels of frames and levels of interdependence that go on in any system, particularly complex behavioral systems such as corporations. This is something that both managers and employees need to take into consideration in order to engage in fruitful problem-solving.

In the case of motivation, when someone attributes causes to their success and/or failure, they may take the attitude that "outside forces" or circumstances that are not directly related influence their goals and expectations. In many cases, this may be true. If a company is undergoing "belt tightening" due to competition or a slow economy, then this may influence the size of an employee's raise. Thus, a low raise would not be the result of poor performance but of patterns evident in a different but connected frame. If this is the case, this information should be shared with the employee so that the attributions are correctly ascribed.

If an outside force is not an influence and yet an employee is constantly blaming "outside forces" for their failure (or success, i.e., "It was just dumb luck that I did so well"), then this needs to be taken into account in the motivating message by emphasizing his ability and effort attributions, and by linking his tasks to his ideas of success and failure.

On the corporate level, outside factors in a larger, more inclusive frame may, indeed, influence performance and results; these could be the market, government policy, war, etc. One frame can, in effect, *inform another frame* and thus alter the parameters set in an adjoining frame. This is the value of "big picture" parallel thinking, mentioned in Chapter 1—you can anticipate the influence of other factors and thus strategically plan for changes.

Another consideration on the corporate level is that of assessing attributions when a particular product or service fails. Let's say you didn't sell the number of widgets you had anticipated and suffer a big loss. The first step is to assess whether your company has the *ability* to effectively manufacture and market the product. If you decide that is the case, then you will want to analyze if sufficient effort was put into all areas involved. If you decide your company does not have the ability to effectively manufacture and market a product—perhaps you are in the high-tech industry and do not have sufficient technical expertise in a certain area—then you will need to decide whether to drop the product, hire for the deficiency, or buy another company that has the ability you need.

Summary

Motivation and criticism should ideally be *ongoing* contexts or *frames* in which all your communication as a manager is delivered. The most productive environment is one in which employees are constantly motivated and criticized in the manners described in this chapter. Motivating and constructively criticizing on an ongoing basis provides employees with the bottom line feedback they need to perform effectively. It can enhance their ongoing performance.

Criticizing and motivating go together. Indeed, both of these messages often do go hand in hand, and for the most powerful message, you want to combine both frames.

It makes intuitive sense to combine the instruction and task orientation of criticism with an employee's personal thoughts about success and failure. The best way to deliver a motivating message is nested in the third step of your criticizing message; that is, the second complimentary/instructive message. At this point, you have fulfilled the two most crucial steps of instructing and of correcting an employee's work-related behavior and you can then deal with the more personal motivating messages.

The table on the next page (Figure 5) will assist you in learning to deliver criticism and motivation in the most effective manner.

At the end of this chapter, you should be able to recognize the difference between motivation and criticism;

- Know the four major components of criticism;
- Know the four major components of motivation;
- Be able to deliver motivation and criticism as a "packaged" message.

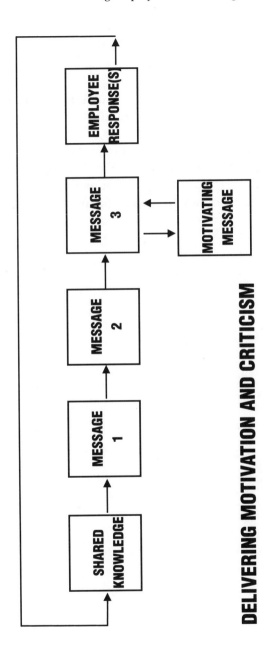

Figure 5

Action Plan

Do the exercises in this chapter.

Devote five minutes each day to assessing your employees' specific tasks; then devote five minutes to assessing their personal ideas of success and failure.

Pick a situation, such as a meeting, in which you can observe how others criticize and motivate. Watch and listen for different communication styles and the reactions that fellow employees have. Analyze how they fit within the model in the chapter.

Relabeling And Reframing

6

New Tools For Managing Context

This chapter will present techniques for altering the components of frames in order to give you powerful tools for changing behavior. The change methods are **Relabeling** and **Reframing**—two related but different techniques.[1]

Relabeling has to do with reinterpreting an experience which has already occurred or been decided upon in some way (it's an after-the-fact tool for change). Reframing, on the other hand, involves figuring out a better way to achieve your goals. It involves intentional change and is pro-active in nature. Reframing requires some forward thinking.

Relabeling

Relabeling is a change technique that you intuitively use all the time. There are three types of relabeling: relabeling by creating positive connotations; relabeling by changing the focus of origins of a problem; and relabeling by substituting a phrase or nominalization which gives a problem situation a more acceptable face-saving interpretation.

Creating Positive Connotations

Relabeling by creating positive connotations is essentially taking any behavior that may be questionable as to whether it's a benefit or a liability and relabeling it as a potentially positive experience. Giving a negative situation positive connotations makes liabilities opportunities.

Oftentimes, if you relabel some experience or attach a new label to a person, they will behave and communicate in ways that are expected of that label (i.e., vice-president versus janitor). This helps to explain the importance of titles and promotions to employees. Upon receipt of a promotion and new title, an employee will often act differently. However, the phenomenon of relabeling communication and behavior is not magic. Psychologist Robert Rosenthal, who has studied "self-fulfilling prophesy" extensively in the area of teacher/student interaction, believes that communication and behavior play a central role in the effectiveness of relabeling. In an article by Lageman (1969), Rosenthal states that:

> "The explanation probably lies in the subtle interaction between teacher and pupils . . . Tone of voice, facial expressions, touch and posture may be the means by which—often unwittingly—she communicates her expectations to her pupils. Such communication may help a child by changing his perceptions of himself."

Self-Fulfilling Prophecy, p. 81.

The analogy of student/teacher (complementary relationship) can be applied to manager/employee relations as well. Relabeling can also be successful between working peers (symmetrical relationships).

Here is an example of relabeling by creating positive connotations. You wanted a promotion within your department. You worked really hard, and you didn't get it. You're disappointed at best. One way to respond might be to say to yourself, "I really wanted that promotion, and it meant a lot to me, but *I can look at it/think about it in another way.* I can look at it as an opportunity to take the time and look at other career paths instead. Maybe this wasn't really the right thing for me to do at this time, and if I look into another area, I will have *even more opportunities* to do the things that I really like to do." That's a general way of taking some negative experience and giving it a positive interpretation. You relabel the experience by giving it positive connotations and thus changing the behavioral response of an employee to a more productive outcome.

You can also relabel over time. For example, a good pattern to establish with employees is to communicate about the employee's performance at regular intervals throughout the year. That has a terrific benefit for the manager. Since you've communicated to the employee throughout the year, the performance appraisal should contain no surprises. It becomes another communication session about work, a building of employee empathy and support (rather than an apprehensive experience) and, as such, gives the appraisal a different label.

Connected to this process is explicitly defining goals and assumptions. If the goals on a job are well-defined, then it's easier to communicate to an employee about what they're doing right or wrong, because they understand specifically what task they are supposed to be doing, and you do too. You have a common agreement about it.

Changing The Focus Of Origins

Changing an identified problem from an individual-generated problem to a group-generated problem is an example of relabeling by shifting the focus of the origins of a problem.

Say that a friend of yours is hired at your company, although not in your department. After several months, he tells you that he feels kind of crummy and isn't getting treated very well, although he can't put his finger on why. You know your friend is a hard worker and an honest person. He has engaged in the behavior of getting to know people, being friendly, and fitting into the culture of that particular department. He is intuitively trying to learn the communication patterns, establish relationships, and do all the normal rituals you do when you start a new job.

However, for all his efforts, he is subtly, nonverbally shunned. The other employees aren't friendly to him and he doesn't get invited out to lunch. When he walks over to the coffee pot to get some coffee, the people standing around talking are suddenly quiet. Someone brings in donuts and he's the only one not offered a donut.

Your friend feels very rejected and upset with this behavior. There are several ways to deal with this. You're out at a bar one evening after work, having a drink, and you say to your friend, Max, "You've been at the company a few months now, how's it going?" He says, "You know, it's really kind of terrible; it's not working out well." He continues, "I really enjoy my tasks, and my boss isn't a bad guy, but I'm not getting along with everyone in the department."

One approach you could use is relabeling by changing the origin of the problem. Max is *personally* feeling badly. He's made the situation an *individual*, personal problem. Relabeling this consists of generalizing the origin of the problem to the larger frame of the *group*, thus making the problem systemic in origin.

You could deliver the relabeling message as a suggestion: "Well, maybe you could look at it this way, Max. Maybe the people have worked in the department together for so long that they're just not used to someone new coming in. It's not really you at all, but just the group dynamics of the situation and the particular culture of that department. You've had enough experience that you realize groups can be really 'cliquey' and it's hard to blend in. Give it some more time."

Another way to deliver the relabeling message is as an assertion: "As a matter of fact, now that I think about it, I've heard of that department before, and it is very insular. A couple of other people I knew who worked there didn't stay long because they got the same response." Again, you're not making it Max's problem. There's nothing wrong with Max. It is the internal communication patterns of the department that are affecting him. This is a common way to reframe a problem in a business setting.

When you relabel a problem in this manner, you change the focus of the problem (from an individual to a group interaction) and attach a different meaning to it. You can keep "enlarging" the frame if necessary and expand the origins of a problem from a group to a larger system such as the "world economy," if the situation calls for it.

Phrase Substitution

As mentioned in Chapter 4, one of the easiest ways to identify a frame is by the use of nominalizations (processes which have been linguistically reorganized into events, i.e., "economy," "inflation," "debt," etc.).

Another way to relabel a problem is by taking one nominalization and replacing it with another which has more positive connotations. You will recognize this pattern as one that is all too commonly used, but powerful nonetheless. The effect of this type of relabeling is automatic reinterpretation coupled with a shift in the goals and assumptions underlying a particular problem.

For example, a layoff is often relabeled a "consolidation of operations"; incurring a loss often becomes "restructuring debt"; termination becomes "early retirement." Such double-speak does not "pass muster" for very long. However, relabeling through shifting nominalizations often buys you time or can be successfully used as a face-saving measure for employees, stockholders, and the public.

A loss by any other name is a loss; however, there is something to relabeling through applying a different nominalization. Goals and priorities will change and a restructuring will occur. Knowing that this process exists, you can intentionally go about changing underlying goals and assumptions when a negative experience occurs.

Such was the case with the "new" Chrysler Corporation. At the edge of insolvency, Chrysler was vastly restructured (that is, relabeled). This included signing new contracts with the auto workers for new financial and work-related goals; divesting of some units for increased cash flow, etc. Thus, if a product or corporation makes systemic changes to its operations, the admonition "new and improved" will indicate that *reframing* has occurred. If underlying goals and assumptions are not changed, then "new and improved" will mean more of the same—the same wine in a new bottle.

The Grinder/Bandler Model

Grinder and Bandler (1982) use what is called "global" relabeling. Their concept of relabeling is based on the idea that *all* behavior is useful at some time for an individual or a corporation. Therefore, problems arise as a result of mismatching between some behavior and the present context. Once this is understood, you need only to generate new, more appropriate solutions to your present problem. This is another way to think about relabeling negative experiences as positive.

Grinder and Bandler's elaborate model involves both relabeling *and* reframing. It gives a problem situation positive connotations and also includes steps which demand that the user figure out better ways to achieve his goals. Refer to their excellent book, *Reframing* (1982) for an entertaining and useful explanation.

Reframing

The word *reframing* is an umbrella term for initiating powerful behavioral changes. There are a variety of ways to reframe a problem and to enact changes with employees and corporations as a whole. These are commonly recognized and often used techniques but are rarely outlined for you. The two areas that will be covered here are *translation* of sensory modalities and *paradoxical techniques.* Each involves reframing in the most general sense of the word and is a powerful, useful pattern of change for your corporation.

In general, reframing is when you shift from one frame of reference to another. The key word here is frame—a system of interaction with its rules, parameters, and notions of stability. The first example to consider is *translation.*

Reframing Through Translating Sensory Modalities

As stated in Chapter 2, a powerful way to establish rapport is by synchronizing your behavior with your fellow employees, especially by matching preferred sensory modalities—literally speaking the language of others.

You can synchronize either by translating your own favored sensory channel to match someone else's, or you can, as a third party, translate between two separate parties (i.e., getting a visually-oriented person who's "envisioning progress" to understand a kinesthetic who's wary of "hitches" and "roadblocks"). Translation of preferred sensory information involves:

1. Self translation of your favored channel to match someone else's;
2. Translation between two or more people separate from yourself.

Both of these are powerful methods of reframing. They involve changing one preferred sensory modality to another. Each preferred sensory modality has its own set of rules that constitute appropriateness and acceptability. What you intuitively call someone's *perspective* is really a reflection of the sensory channel they prefer to use to process and represent information. Employees often make choices based on their PSM; thus, if you learn which *words* and *phrases* an employees uses to express his favored sensory modality, you can learn to *match* preferred representational systems. In addition, you can learn to verbally *translate* between visual, kinesthetic, or auditory frames of reference.

Being able to translate sensory channels has many benefits for day-to-day job performance. You can:

1. Translate work-related tasks and duties into the favored sensory channel of each employee, thus establishing rapport and increasing the amount of high quality information an employee receives;
2. Translate between others so that each individual on a team can better understand each other's perspective and frame of reference. This will also increase your personal influence with your team members.

A good team or program leader often unconsciously has developed this type of reframing ability that makes him stand out as a versatile, effective leader.

The following is a translation table developed by John Grinder and Richard Bandler (1976) for the purposes of demonstrating how to translate the various sensory modes:

TRANSLATION TABLE

Meaning	Kinesthetic	Visual	Auditory
I don't understand you	What you are saying feels (doesn't feel) right to me	I see (don't see) what you are saying	I hear (don't hear) you clearly
I want to communicate something to you	I want you to be in touch with something	I want to show you something (a picture of something)	I want you to listen carefully to what I say to you
Describe more of your present experience to me	Put me in touch with what you are feeling at this point in time	Show me a clear picture of what you see at this point in time	Tell me in more detail what you are saying at this time
I like my experience of you and me at this point in time	This feels really good to me. I feel really good about...	This looks really bright and clear to me	This sounds really good to me
Do you understand what I am saying?	Does what I am putting you in touch with feel...?	Do you see what I am showing you?	Does what I am saying sound right to you?

Source: *The Structure of Magic, Vol. II,* p. 15.

One example of the power of this type of reframing can be found in the context of sales. Dr. Donald Moine (1982) has studied patterns of successful salespeople for several years. He discovered that highly successful salespeople intuitively "speak the language" of their customers. That is, they translate from their own favored modality to that of their clients, creating instant empathy.

Suppose a high-level manager needs to have information gathered on an important project. He delegates the task to three of his managers. They, in turn, gather the pieces of information and integrate them into a report. Joe, a visual, goes to his people and asks for a graph and written memo. Max, an auditory, explains the situation to his people and asks for a verbal reply. Bruno, a kinesthetic, tells his people to walk through his area and come back and give him a feel for where the problems in the plant are. Although all three are gathering data, each uses a different sensory-based method.

In order to avoid a clash of styles, costly delays, and lowered productivity, the high-level manager needs to translate each of the different sensory-based sets of information toward a common format, as follows:

"Bruno, I understand that you have a good *feel* for what's going on out on the line. I need you to take that information and *explain* it to Max. Max, I need you to take what *you've heard* and what Bruno *tells* you and *explain* it to Joe so that he can get a *clear picture* of the problem and *write up a report*. Joe, I need you to *see* what Max and Bruno are *saying* and get it *written down*."

Here the high-level manager has read each manager's preferred sensory modality and given accurate feedback to each. This exercise in reframing through translation can greatly assist managers and employees alike in getting the job done more efficiently and productively.

Exercise 11

Find a short company-produced letter, memo, notice, newsletter, etc., and:

1. Find three paragraphs which use words that specify PSM such as *look, see* (visual), *touch, feel* (kinesthetic), and *listen, hear* (auditory);
2. Then translate the paragraphs from one PSM to another by rewriting the words and phrases that indicate visual, auditory, and kinesthetic sensory experience;
3. Note which sensory modality is easiest for you to write in and which is most difficult. Check your results with Exercise 1.

This exercise gives you practice in reframing from one sensory modality to another and also has the effect of highlighting your weaknesses and strengths with respect to translating the vocabulary of the senses.

Reframing Through Paradox

Many times you need to employ communication techniques that appear odd or illogical or paradoxical in nature. These techniques are not only applied interpersonally but also organizationally because there are impasses within organizations that demand more sophisticated approaches to problem-solving.

Here is an example of paradoxical communication. There is a typical pattern Americans use when they're speaking to someone who is not fluent in English. They ask a question such as, "Excuse me, do you know where the bathroom is in this hotel?" Of course, the other person doesn't understand, but this does not deter the American from paradoxical persistence. They repeat the same question only *louder! And* they expect the other person to miraculously understand the second time.

Another common work-related problem involves employees who won't talk about their work when they need to. The most common response to an employee who isn't talking is to *try to talk them into talking*, which is the same as yelling at the foreigner in English. You have a multi-level problem and you're using a narrow, one-level solution. You may instead want to try using techniques that are paradoxical and that involve solving the problem on more than one level of analysis.

Sarcastic remarks or events that are slightly out of place are often paradoxical in nature. Suppose I bump into someone and say, "Excuse me, I'm sorry." He responds by saying, "Don't be so polite." This is a contradictory sort of response.

Paradoxical problem-solving is *habit-* or *frame-breaking*. It is the *intentional* altering of the components of frames. Before you've learned about the problems that occur when you unintentionally violate rules of communication. Now, you can learn that there are situations where you can make changes in people and organizations by *intentionally* breaking the communication rules. (This presupposes that you are aware of the person's or organization's behavioral patterns.)

If you are at a point in a work situation where you've tried to establish rapport through normal channels and that hasn't worked, then you may want to use paradoxical techniques.

Reframing through paradox operates from the concept of presupposition. You need to identify the beliefs which underlie the behavior of the person you are dealing with. Often, the issues will be ones of relationship and control between you and the employee.

There are two types of paradoxical reframing which are most useful in business contexts: *exaggeration* and *behavioral prescription*. A third, restraining, is also powerful and is discussed at length in the context of therapy in Weeks and L'Abate (1982).

Paradoxical Case 1: The Employee "Shut Down" (Reframing Through Exaggeration)

Some employees "shut down" when under stress. Their posture becomes rigid, they rarely talk to anyone, and they don't alter their facial expressions.

The first step in using any change technique is to make the person feel all right about themselves, regardless of whether they're doing something that may be annoying to you or not. Don't be concerned at this point with "why" they are doing the behavior. What you're concerned with in terms of change and communication is (1) recognizing the behavior as a technique for coping with stress and (2) accepting that coping mechanism. This is part of the process of identifying the presupposition which underlies the behavior. You do that by establishing empathy and accepting the behavior nonverbally and/or verbally ("I accept the way that you cope with this"). The person will automatically begin to open up.

If *your* mechanism for coping with stress is to "shut down" and someone indicates verbally or nonverbally that the way you cope with stress is bad, what's that going to do? It may encourage you to shut down even more. It becomes a vicious cycle.

You want to accept some behaviors regardless of the consequences of how you think about them. If someone behaves the way you behave, that's a covert form of acceptance, mirroring, establishing empathy and support. The first step of paradoxical exaggeration is to *mirror* the "shutting down" behavior and then *exaggerate* it slightly. That creates an opportunity for the employee to become aware of the problem behavior and thus gain control. The employee responds because the message is a little bit more than what he is already doing. It makes him conscious of it and breaks the cycle he was caught in.

Exaggeration is based on the concept of threshold. It's as simple as not being able to hear the radio at five, so you turn it to six. More specifically, it's based on the concept of receivable *sensory* threshold.

Some people can tolerate watching a movie that's slightly out of focus. Some people have to have it crystal clear. Some people, if you touch them with a certain pressure, won't feel it, and others will. When people say, "Someone's in the room" or "I can feel someone" many times they're picking up on acoustic (auditory) or tactile information that they're not consciously aware of.

In the case of the "shut down" employee, by acting even more rigid and silent than them, you frustrate them into opening up. It's a paradoxical way of giving them support and control.

Paradoxical Case 2: The Tardy Employee (Reframing Through Prescription)

Let's say you have an employee (Max) who, for a long time, has been coming in late. It really bothers you when your employees are late; you take it personally. You've tried the patterns of communication from Chapter 2. You have tried establishing rapport and asking if there is some kind of problem or any way you can help Max. Max is very obstinate and won't talk about any problems that are making him late. Maybe he really dislikes you and he's depressed about having to come to work. Or maybe he can't stand his tasks, and you've reassigned his job a couple of times, and that hasn't worked either. You're at the point where you're really going to get tough.

An alternative strategy at this point might be to try a paradoxical reframing technique (rather than going to industrial relations and saying, "This guy is a total pain; how do I initiate termination procedures?"). Try something new; prescribe the problem behavior, this way:

"Max, I realize that you've been late quite a bit, and I want you to know that it's really okay with me that you're late. As a matter of fact, if you want to be even later than you are, that's perfectly all right with me as long as you get your work done."

In order for this technique to work, you need to have identified the underlying presupposition with respect to Max's tardiness, specifically how he feels about authority (or "one-up/one-down" complementary relationships).

Max is disobeying and not following authority. He's not being a "good worker" and he's flaunting his obstinance by being insubordinate (rejecting authority). That's the frame you've defined. When you, as a manager, condone the behavior vis-a-vis prescribing it, it changes the frame and redefines the behavior for the employee. He can no longer be disobedient and get what he wants. This often puts him on guard in some way and forces him to shift his problem behavior. That's what you want. After all, you've tried to discipline him in the traditional manner and he didn't pay any attention to that. As soon as you tell Max that what he's doing is okay, you create a situation where in order for him to disobey you, he now has to do what *you* want instead of what he wants.

In this situation, you often have an employee with an authority problem as the underlying belief or presupposition. The employee may automatically disobey what you ask him to do (be late). By disobeying, he will perform the correct behavior that you want him to do. You've established contact with the employee at a deep level by binding him with a paradoxical injunction. This often results in a confusing but self-enriching "ah ha" experience for the employee.

Paradox and Punishment

Most people respond to behavior they don't like by trying to stop it with some form of punishment—they order someone to stop doing what they're doing or tell them to go away.

The common example of tardiness is one that is frequently dealt with by orders ("Don't be late") and threats ("I'm not going to give you a raise"). This is a "beat a dead horse" approach to trying to solve a complex, multi-level problem.

An example of a single-level change is the process known as progressive discipline. This is a series of steps where there's an identified "problem employee" and an *escalating series of punishments executed within the same frame.*

At the point when you initiate progressive discipline, you assume that either the person is going to leave the company or you're going to try to terminate them.

Another way to approach the behavior is to *prescribe* it to the employee until corrective, frame-changing behavior occurs. As a manager, you challenge not the overt behavior of the employee's tardiness, but the relationship you have with the employee. Another way of putting this is that you condone the *symptom* (tardiness) in the hope of affecting the underlying *cause* (a problem with authority-related complementary relationships). Frame-breaking change, then, means the indirect addressing of a belief or presupposition a person has of which an overt behavior is only the symptom. Through paradoxical prescriptions, you can bring the unconscious belief to the surface by breaking an old habit or defense mechanism. The effect is that the employee gains control over the previously unconscious behavior and can work toward positive, productive changes.

Exercise 12

Think of some action which you would normally have a severe negative reaction to and prescribe some sort of punishment in order to change. Then:

1. Imagine the results that the punishment might have;
2. Imagine the results that prescribing the negative action might have as opposed to the punishment.

Exercise 12 is an opportunity for you to think about problems and their solutions in a paradoxical manner. It is intended to conceptually expand your approach to solving work-related problems.

Summary

Chapter Six introduces you to frame-altering change techniques. Here you take a variety of aspects of behavior and reinterpret them in a new, more useful way, or change them altogether toward a more productive goal/outcome. Specifically, you learned:

1. Relabeling behavior;
2. Reframing behavior.

Each of these forms of frame-changing can be used along with all the other tools in this book to enact powerful changes in work-related behavior.

At the end of this chapter you should be able to engage the following change patterns:

- Relabel negatively perceived communication as positive and beneficial in at least one respect;
- Relabel an individually perceived problem as a group/ organizational problem;
- Reframe an individual's perspective through translating from one preferred sensory modality to another;
- Exaggerate some identified problem communication so that an individual can gain control of the identified communication pattern;
- Paradoxically reconceptualize a problem where punishment as a solution might normally be involved.

Action Plan

Do the exercise in this chapter.

Devote one minute of a conversation each day to listening for the words that indicate a person's preferred sensory modality.

Pick one negative experience per week that someone who works with you has described, and relabel the experience by ascribing some positive, alternative evaluation to it.

Negotiation 7

Toward Mutually Beneficial Outcomes

Negotiation is integrating two or more separate frames of reference toward mutually beneficial outcomes—mutually aligning your goals with someone else's.

For example, suppose you are going to buy a new computer for your business. You are going to enter into a negotiation about the price, what is included in the price, and perhaps the delivery time. The outcome that both you and the salesman want will drive the negotiation. In this case, you may want a good computer that does what the salesman say it does and can be serviced when you need it to be—all at a fair and reasonable price. The salesman may want to make a decent profit, to capture you as a repeat customer, create good will and hope that you will refer other business associates to him.

Thus, the salesman will want the product to work for you and guarantee excellent service so that you and your associates come back for more products. Here is a case where the buying and selling *frames* overlap/merge around mutually beneficial goals. The driving goal in this case might be "creating good will" for the purposes of providing good service and for capturing repeat business.

Along the path of merging your goals and desired outcomes toward some common ground, you will test all the elements which define the frame or context in which you're operating. All your communication and relationship-building skills may be challenged.

Negotiation not only occurs between people and companies,

butbetween people in the same company as well. Employees and managers in large corporations often say, "You know, sometimes I wonder if we all work for the same company around here; with all the fighting and lack of cooperation, it's amazing anything gets done at all!" Getting the job done effectively involves doing a good job of negotiating.

As discussed in Chapter 4, a common conflict occurs between manufacturing and engineering operations. This is a case where two conflicting frames need to be integrated so that the product can get out the door, and a good profit realized. No one in either the manufacturing or engineering organizations would deny that there are mutually beneficial outcomes that each organization desires. Each wants to make a profit so they can stay in business, deliver the product in a timely manner, guarantee a certain level of quality and customer service, manufacture at a low cost, and continue to develop the product.

Even with these driving goals, managers and employees often do not experience their day-to-day operations as a harmonious team working toward mutually beneficial outcomes. Individuals and organizations fail in making these desired outcomes explicit and in negotiating for the behaviors and resources they need. Let's look at a model of how to negotiate for mutually beneficial outcomes which reduces conflict and increases productivity.

Steps For Negotiating Mutually Beneficial Outcomes[1]

Negotiation generally involves five steps which, if practiced, will increase the chances that both you and your counterparts will get what you want and need. This will hold true whether the negotiation frame is *one-on-one* (e.g., you and your boss negotiating a pay raise); *company to company* (e.g., one corporation negotiating with another for acquisition of real property); or *two nations* (e.g., negotiating for arms control).

The five steps are:

1. Preparing for the negotiation;
2. Generating a list of desired outcomes or goals (both yours and your counterparts);
3. Comparing the two lists of outcomes/goals and asking yourself: "Where is there overlap? What are the differences?"
4. Separating individual communication from the outcomes you want to achieve so as to minimize potential for personality and cultural clashes;
5. Developing a method of *accountability* for measuring compliance with the agreements of the negotiation.

1—Prepare For Negotiation

There is no substitute for a well-prepared negotiation. You cannot "wing it" and expect to achieve your desired outcomes.

Generally, negotiation preparation involves gathering information or facts:

- related to your goals; and
- related to the people involved in the actual negotiation.

You can influence the outcome of the negotiation better by thinking through all the possible goals and assumptions related to a negotiation and all the people-related communication and relationship issues. Let's look at a brief example of what this phase might entail.

Sample Case 1: Preparing For Negotiation

In their excellent book, *Getting To Yes* (1981), authors Fisher and Ury encapsulate the prenegotiation process as follows:

"During the *analysis* stage you are simply trying to diagnose the situation—to gather information, organize it, and think about it. You will want to consider the people problems of partisan perceptions, hostile emotions, and unclear communication, as well as to identify your interests and those of the other side. You will want to note options already on the table and identify any criteria already suggested as a basis for agreement.

During the *planning* stage you deal with the same four elements a second time, both generating ideas and deciding what to do. How do you propose to handle the people problems? Of your interests, which are most important? And what are some realistic objectives? You will want to generate additional options and additional criteria for deciding among them.

Again, during the *discussion* stage, when the parties communicate back and forth, looking toward agreement, the same four elements are the best subjects to discuss. Differences in perception, feelings of frustration and anger, and difficulties in communication can be acknowledged and addressed. Each side should come to understand the interests of the other. Both can then jointly generate options that are mutually advantageous and seek agreement on objective standards for resolving opposed interests."

Getting To Yes, pp. 12-14.

Here is an example of the prenegotiation process.

Max and Roscoe are managers from roughly same size companies. Max works for the ABC Co. which makes semiconductors, test equipment, and other high-tech measurement and electronic devices. Roscoe works for the XYZ Co. which also makes high-tech equipment; computers, software, and telecommunications. Max wants to sell Roscoe some semiconductors for his company's new minicomputer. Roscoe wants the kind of semiconductors that Max's company produces for, understandably, as cheaply as he can get them. *Here are two outcomes which need to be integrated.*

Max and Roscoe are in the preparation phase of negotiation. Max knows that Roscoe needs the chips in a fairly short amount of time, as XYZ's main competitor has just announced that they will be coming out with a similar minicomputer about the same time as XYZ would like to.

At this point, Max and Roscoe have some understanding of

the data related to the goals of the negotiation. They also have made some assumptions about this particular frame. Max assumes that Roscoe will want the chips as cheaply as possible, and as soon as possible due to competition. Roscoe assumes that Max's company can make the chips he needs in the desired quantity and in the desired time-frame. *All of these assumptions may, in fact, be false.* As a matter of fact, if Max and Roscoe leave even one of their assumptions unchecked either beforehand or at the negotiation table, disaster can occur.

Thus, one key aspect of formulating a strategy within the negotiation frame is to generate an outline of *all* your desired outcomes and assumptions with respect to the company, products, and individuals involved. Each goal and assumption should be shared as common knowledge to your negotiation team and then put across the table to your counterparts. There are many times when an assumption proves to be false, or a goal cannot be met, necessitating a recalibration of your goals and assumptions and forcing a shift in the parameters of your frame.

For example, Max was sure that Roscoe needed the chips ASAP because XYZ's competitors are coming out with a rival model computer. Therefore, Max was going to use time pressure to force Roscoe to accept a higher price on his chips. In more formal terms, Max was going to manipulate the communication variable of *time* against the variable of *price* to achieve his company's desired outcome of maximizing profit. However, unknown to Max, Roscoe's company is willing—for a limited amount of time—to divert the identical chips from an "in-house" project which does not have the same time-frame pressure to get the product to market. Thus, Max cannot as effectively use this type of tactic to reach his company's goals. He will need to be flexible and have generated other options.

Another key aspect of prenegotiation is assessing the relationships of the people involved. In this case, Max and Roscoe are both mid-level managers from similarly sized companies. Their relative status and influence will be approximately formal-symmetrical. Each has a "final" price they can agree on as well as control over time, delivery, legal terms, etc. Relationship, however, is another parameter which can be altered and thus affect negotiation outcomes.

For example, a mid-level manager in a large company may have as much or more control over a project or product as the president of a small corporation. Thus, in order to "get things done," a mid-level manager from a large corporation may *have* to do all his negotiating with the president of a small corporation. Any other person may not have the "final say" about a project or product. Going into negotiation without the counterparts being symmetrical, with respect to control and influence, can cause costly delays, frustration and poor negotiation.

As stated in Chapter 3, there are clues as to what kind of relationships you have with fellow employees, and relationships that the people on the opposing negotiating team have with each other. For example, if you are leading negotiations for your company and need to defer to members of your team for certain information, your nonverbal communication will be assessed by the other team, albeit unconsciously. Although you may be in a formal-complementary relationship with certain members of your team, you may have an informal-symmetrical relationship with other members. As a result, you may be judged (rightly or wrongly) as not having the "real" power on your team, or not having the crucial facts or final say. Such a judgement could jeopardize your role and ability to meet the parameters of the contract you are negotiating.

Another limiting factor may be the rules of the corporate culture you are negotiating within. For example, although Max and Roscoe are apparently formally-symmetrical, Roscoe's corporate hierarchy dictates that he call his headquarters and consult with his boss (a vice-president) before making any final decisions. Behind the scenes, Roscoe is informally-complementary ("one-down") to Max.

Having to defer to a higher-up is neither an advantage nor disadvantage in and of itself. It is another parameter which Max and Roscoe need to know in order to calibrate and recalibrate their respective negotiation tactics. For example, if Max knows that Roscoe must defer to his boss at corporate headquarters, then he can build this time delay into his negotiation strategy and not be pressured into giving in on any aspect of the contract.

Another aspect of prenegotiation to consider is the use of communication style—yours *and* theirs. A negotiating session will involve a myriad of rules about posture, gestures, what can and cannot be said, time, space, sensory preference and manipulation, thinking styles, etc. Subtle verbal and nonverbal clues may indicate changes in relationship, shift of resolve and sureness of negotiating position. Patterns of ethnic/cultural communication may signal the acceptance or abrupt termination of a contract.

Finally, you'll need to consider communication strategies. Suppose Roscoe is highly visual and a serial thinker—a lover of details, facts, and figures. From a negotiating point of view, one tactic Max could take is pattern matching—synchronizing with Roscoe's communication style, specifically his visual PSM and his serial PTS. Max would then, to the greatest extent possible, synchronize his presentation, providing visual input for Roscoe, visual language, and lots of detail. With this approach, Max may be able to engage Roscoe by creating product empathy and rapport with him at the initial states of negotiation. From this point, Max may want to *modulate* his communication style to bluff or buy time.

Return of Cultural Factors

As mentioned in Chapter 1, ethnicity and accompanying cultural habits and politics can be an influence in the "do's and don't's" of communication. Nowhere is this more evident than in international negotiations. Many times, a country's mores, history and larger cultural heritage influence it's goals, attitudes, and approaches to such factors as time and rapport. Thus, a necessity in international or interethnic negotiation is to plan to acquire as much cultural knowledge and perspective as possible so that the inevitable faux pas is not so inevitable.

The Remaining Steps

Let's go over the remaining steps involved in the negotiation process. Your ability to influence the outcome of a negotiation is a factor of your communication effectiveness and also your ability to analyze and blend contexts toward a common goal. The remaining steps in the negotiation process assist you in putting integrating frames into practice.

2—Generate A List of Desired Outcomes

Successful negotiation involves generating (brainstorming) two lists of desired goals/outcomes—yours *and* your counterpart's. In order to increase the chances of successfully integrating your desired outcomes with someone else's, you need a plurality of goals to draw upon. For example, an international negotiation over arms control may involve several mutually beneficial goals—security, peace, cultural exchange, shifts in economic priorities, international respect, etc. The more mutually beneficial outcomes you have to draw on, the easier it will be for you to create common ground between parties. Having more than one or two major goals gives you, the negotiator, increased flexibility and more room to maneuver.

3—Compare The Two Lists of Outcomes/Goals To Discover Overlap And Difference

This process sets the parameters of the negotiation frame. Lining up similarities and differences lets you know specifically where there may be conflict and resolution. If you need to figure out what you can "swap" or trade, this is the step which will assist you in coming up with your "bargaining chips."

4—Separate Individual Communication From The Outcomes You Want To Achieve

Focus on the task to be accomplished, not the personalities involved. You probably have had an experience where you had to work with someone else on a task, and you both had mutually beneficial goals, but you couldn't stand the person. There was a total clash of communication styles. He was abrasive and you were calm and collected. In this type of situation, it is easy to lose sight of your goals and get involved in personality conflicts. By utilizing all of the communication tools in this book *and* staying focused on your goals, you will minimize costly, unproductive interpersonal boxing matches.

You will need to be synchronized in regard to communication, relationships, and desired outcomes. Data, mood, power, and follow-through all need to be explicitly agreed upon, otherwise the negotiation will most likely fail, or the final outcome be delayed. If you and your counterpart are not in a symmetrical relationship in regard to decision-making, then an entire negotiation session could be subverted by political machinations from headquarters. This not only puts the contract in jeopardy, it creates mistrust and lack of rapport. It the two main counterparts (or any of their team members) have openly conflicting communication styles, animosity can be created. The unsynchronized behaviors need to be resolved so that further animosity does not fester and aspects of negotiation unravel. Synchronized behavior in the closing phase of a negotiation is the *essence of excellent customer service and relations.* Also, targeted goals need to be reiterated and mutually agreed upon before signing your deal.

5—Develop A Method of Accountability

In order to assure that your negotiated outcomes are maintained, you need to develop a method of accountability. Some methods of accountability are common and everyday—a product *warranty,* for example, is a device to assure accountability.

Another common form of accountability is the process of *inspection.* An arms agreement between two countries may require "on site" inspection for compliance. This makes each country accountable to the terms (goals/outcomes) of a negotiated arms deal.

On an individual basis, methods of performance evaluation/appraisal should be situations whereby management and employees make each other accountable for employee performance. Often this is not the case because Steps 2 through 4 of the negotiation model have been ignored—with disastrous consequences. One remedy to the performance appraisal process is for the manager to take a leadership role and enact mutual goal-setting and contracts for employee accountability (frame-changing behavior).

Your overall strategy in the accountability phase is to engage in rapport-building behavior which enhances customer relations, employee relations, service, and inter- and intra-company productivity. Two corporations working toward rapport-building communication have much the same outcome as rapport-building inside a company. Productivity is enhanced, employees are motivated, mistakes and confusion are minimized. Therefore, a proper negotiation session involves using many of the same communication tools discussed in this book.

The Signs of Successful Negotiation

How do you know when a successful negotiation has occurred? Some of the signs are:

1. Trust and rapport between parties have been established; synchronized behavior is occurring;
2. Both parties are speaking a common language revolving around their agreed upon goals/desired outcomes;
3. Both parties are congruent in their referral to their goals;
4. A system of mutually agreed upon feedback (accountability) has been established.

Once opposing parties function like a *team*, indicating that the two once separate but overlapping contexts have integrated, linked by one or more mutually beneficial outcomes, then you will know your negotiation has been successful.

Exercise 13

Imagine that you have just been informed that you are to negotiate a $4 million contract with a corporation twice the size of yours. The contract is very complex, involving both finished products and services. You are to imagine setting up a mock negotiation from two points of view: one as the procurer of the product/services and one as the seller of the product/services. You may imagine using any product/service combination that you are familiar with.

Make a list going through all the steps outlined in this chapter regarding prenegotiation, accountability, etc. Your task is to create two sets of desired outcomes, two communication and relationship profiles—one for you and one for your counterpart. Simulate on paper the setting as best you can.

Exercise 14

After setting up a negotiation session on paper, approach it from the following points of view:

Scenario 1: Imagine that time is not a problem. You have many weeks to close the deal.
Scenario 2: Imagine that "time is of the essence." You have a strict deadline and are under a great deal of pressure.

Outline how your tactics and accompanying behaviors might change with respect to the two scenarios. What would you do the same or different?

Summary

Negotiation involves the merging of two sometimes conflicting "realities" or contexts. Whereas most negotiation is characterized in war-like adversarial terms, the model here presents how win-win negotiation can occur. In fact, unless both sides realize mutually beneficial and agreed upon outcomes, the negotiation will fail.

The key to successful negotiation is not in rough-and-tumble behavior or the excess abuse of power—it relies on careful preparation, rapport-building, and explicit knowledge of goals and limits. Generating more than one desired outcome through traditional brainstorming techniques allows for more than a single choice to be possible. This flexibility is the key to successful maneuvering and influencing others to your desired goals.

At the end of this chapter, you should be able to:

• Generate a list of mutually beneficial outcomes for you and your negotiation counterparts;
• Know the three steps to successful negotiation;
• Develop methods of accountability.

Action Plan

Do the exercises in this chapter.

Devote five minutes each day to outlining from memory all the communication information you can recall about a person you have previously negotiated a contract, deal, or sale with.

Discover a contract/sale negotiation at your company/job which was successful and one which was unsuccessful. Do some background research and try to find out the differences between the two and link those differences to the outcome.

Afterword

Making The Message Clear

Making The Message Clear provides you with powerful tools for managing drawn from a variety of fields in the behavioral sciences. The first four chapters provide you with a way of organizing your management and work experience so that you can recognize many of the ways in which problems originate and then can be resolved. Chapters 5-7 demonstrate specific tools you can use in a variety of contexts to enhance employee behavior toward more productive and job-enriching ends.

As a final tool for making important decisions about job-related tasks, please note the diagram below:

All decisions occur in a context or frame and their success or failure (and thus your success or failure) depend on excellent judgement. So remember that to make the message clear for improved productivity and morale, always include management communication, employee communication, and the goals/ desired outcome of each in the decision-making process.

Footnotes

Chapter 1

1. For further reading regarding this fascinating and influential field, the reader is advised to consult *Frogs Into Princes* by Richard Bandler and John Grinder; *Neurolinguistic Programming, Vol. I* by Robert Dilts, John Grinder, et al., and *Using Your Brain For A Change* by Richard Bandler (cf. References).
2. For a slightly different albeit related view of serial and parallel processing in business, read *How Manager's Minds Work* by J. McKenney and P. Keen (cf. References).
3. John Grinder and Richard Bandler's *Trance-Formations* offers an excellent account of the use of metaphor in communication for those interested.

Chapter 2

1. For a more in-depth discussion of the use of cognitive strategies in communication, refer to *Neurolinguistic Programming, Vol. I* (op. cit.), This also includes a discussion of assessing PSM vis-a-vis vertical and lateral eye movements.
2. Excellent examples of the use of negative and positive reinforcement in communication can be found in Section Two on *Anchoring* in *Frogs Into Princes* (op. cit.), in *The One Minute Manager* by K. Blanchard and S. Johnson, and in *Putting The One Minute Manager To Work* by K. Blanchard and R. Lorber (cf. References).
3. See Paul Hersey's *Situational Selling* for an excellent example of how to use rapport-building in the context of sales (cf. References).

Chapter 3

1. For a brilliant discussion of the varieties of human interaction and evolution, the reader is encouraged to consult Gregory Bateson's *Steps To An Ecology Of Mind*. The ideas of symmetrical and complementary relationships originated with Bateson's work in anthropology and is discussed in the above cited work, Part Two, article one.

Also confer B. Oncken's excellent *Managing Management Time* for a discussion of relationships and time management (cf. References).

Chapter 4

1. For a stimulating discussion of the nature of context in human communication, read *Steps To An Ecology Of Mind*, Sections Two, Three, Four, and Five (op. cit.).
2. I define an assumption as an unexpressed or uncommunicated goal.

Chapter 5

1. The ideas concerning motivation and attribution in this chapter are from the seminal work of Bernard Weiner and his associates at the University of California at Los Angeles. Readers are urged to consult Weiner's "Principles For a Theory of Student Motivation And Their Application In An Attributional Framework" and Sandra Graham's "Teacher Feelings and Student Thoughts" for further reading in this important area (cf. References).

Chapter 6

1. For in-depth discussions of reframing and relabeling from a variety of perspectives, the reader should consult *Paradoxical Psychotherapy* by G. Weeks and L. L'Abate; *Reframing* by R. Bandler and J. Grinder; and *Change* by P. Watzlawick (cf. References).

Chapter 7

1. Both Fisher and Ury's *Getting To Yes* and Grinder and McMaster's *Precision* offer excellent models of negotiation for those desiring additional discussion (cf. References).

References

Bandler, Richard. *Using Your Brain*. Utah: Real People Press, 1985.

Bandler, Richard and John Grinder. *Frogs Into Princes*. Utah: Real People Press, 1979.

Bandler, Richard and John Grinder. *Reframing*. Utah: Real People Press, 1982.

Bandler, Richard and John Grinder. *The Structure of Magic, Vol. I*. Palo Alto: Science And Behavior Books, 1975.

Bateson, Gregory. *Steps To An Ecology Of Mind*. New York: Ballantine Books, 1972.

Bennis, Warren and Burt Nanus. *Leaders*. New York: Harper And Row, 1985.

Blanchard, Ken and Spencer Johnson. *The One Minute Manager*. New York: Morrow, 1982.

Blanchard, Kenneth and Robert Lorber. *Putting The One Minute Manager To Work*. New York: Morrow, 1984.

Block, Peter. *The Empowered Manager*. San Francisco: Jossey-Bass, 1987.

Deal, Terrence and Allan Kennedy. *Corporate Cultures*. Reading: Addison-Wesley, 1982.

Dilts, Robert and John Grinder, et. al. *Neurolinguistic Programming, Vol. I*. Cupertino: Meta Publications, 1980.

Eicher, James. "Linguistics and the Problem of Serial Order." *Papers in Linguistics*, v. 10, 1-2, Spring/Summer, 1977.

Eicher, James, John Jones and William Bearley. *Neurolinguistic Communication Profile*. King of Prussia, PA: Organization Design and Development, 1990.

Eicher, James, John Jones and William Bearley. *Rapport: Matching and Mirroring Communication*. King of Prussia, PA: Organization Design and Development, 1990.

Fisher, Roger and William Ury. *Getting To Yes*. Boston: Houghton Mifflin, 1981.

Gardner, Howard. *Frames of Mind.* New York: Basic Books, 1985.

Goleman, Daniel. "People Who Read People." *Psychology Today,* July 1979.

Graham, Sandra. "Teacher Feelings And Student Thoughts." *The Elementary School Journal,* University of Chicago Press, Volume 85, No. 1., 1984.

Grinder, John and Richard Bandler. *The Structure of Magic, Vol. II.* Palo Alto: Science And Behavior Books, 1976.

Grinder, John and Richard Bandler. *Trance-Formations.* Utah: Real People Press, 1981.

Hall, Edward and William Whyte. "Intercultural Communication." *Human Organization,* Vol. 19, No. 1, 1960, in Leavitt, R., et. al., Readings In Managerial Psychology, 1979.

Hersey, Paul. *The Situational Leader.* Escondido, CA: Center For Leadership Studies, 1984.

Hersey, Paul. *Situational Selling.* Escondido, CA: Center For Leadership Studies, 1984.

Lageman, John. "Self-Fulfilling Prophecy--A Key To Success." *The Reader's Digest,* Feb. 1969.

LeDoux, Joseph E. and William Hirst. *Mind and Brain: Dialogues in Cognitive Neuroscience.* Cambridge: University of Cambridge Press, 1986.

McCall, Morgan and Michael Lombardo, "What Makes A Top Executive?" *Psychology Today,* Feb. 1983.

McCaskey, Michael. "The Hidden Message Managers Send." *Harvard Business Review,* Nov.-Dec., 1979.

McKenney, J. and P. Keen. "How Manager's Minds Work." *Harvard Business Review,* 1974, in Leavitt, R., et. al., *Readings In Managerial Psychology,* 1979.

McMaster, Michael and John Grinder. *Precision.* Cupertino, CA: Meta Publications, 1980.

Moine, Donald. "Irresistible Information." *Pharmaceutical Representative,* June, 1982.

Norman, Donald. *The Design of Everyday Things.* New York: Doubleday, 1988.

Oncken, Jr., William. *Managing Management Time*. New Jersey: Prentice Hall, 1984.

Ouchi, William. *Theory Z*. Reading: Addison-Wesley, 1981.

Peters, Thomas and Robert Waterman. *In Search of Excellence*. New York: Warner Books, 1982.

Watzlawick, Paul. *How Real Is Real?* New York: Vintage Books, 1977.

Watzlawick, Paul, et. al. *Change*. New York: Norton, 1974.

Watzlawick, Paul, et. al. *Pragmatics of Human Communication*. New York: Norton, 1967.

Weeks, Gerald and Luciano L'Abate. *Paradoxical Psychotherapy*. New York: Brunner/Mazel, 1982.

Weiner, Bernard. "Principles For a Theory of Student Motivation and Their Application Within An Attributional Framework." In Ames, Russell, and Ames, Carole (ed.), *Research On Motivation In Education*. New York: Academic Press, 1984.

Williams, Linda. *Teaching For The Two-Sided Mind*. New Jersey: Prentice-Hall, 1983.

About The Author

Jim Eicher is the creator of Cognitive Management™, a theory of management which applies research from the cognitive sciences to organization and management behavior. Jim has also authored *Making The Message Clear*, a highly acclaimed book on management and communication, as well as the training programs *Empowering Communication*™, *Building Customer Rapport*™, and *Reframing: Communication For A Change*. Jim is also featured in the video program *Meeting The Communication Challenge*.

Many of the tools presented in *Making The Message Clear* are based on the exciting and innovative field of Neurolinguistic Programming (NLP). NLP was developed in the 1970s by John Grinder and Richard Bandler to understand the communication processes of high achieving individuals. Jim was one of Grinder and Bandler's original "whiz kids" who assisted with the development and implementation of early NLP. He has refined and enhanced the original theory to now provide a complete, practical model of communication and change.

A dynamic and humorous speaker, Jim has taught numerous seminars for Northrop Corp., *The Los Angeles Times*, Hughes Aircraft Company, Amdahl Corp., Philips, Levi Strauss, National Semiconductor, AC Transit, Abbott Labs, and the University of California, among others. He holds a Bachelor's degree in Theoretical Linguistics from the University of California, Santa Cruz, and a Master's degree in Educational Psychology from the University of California, Los Angeles. Jim is available for training, program certification, keynote presentations, and executive coaching. He can be contacted at 1063 Morse Ave., #9-309, Sunnyvale, CA 94089 (408) 744-1332.

For More Information

James Eicher has also developed a series of training instruments and leader guides on NLP with Dr. John E. Jones and Dr. William L. Bearley, *The Neurolinguistic Communication Profile* and *Rapport: Matching and Mirroring Communication.*

The training programs *Building Customer Rapport*™ and *Empowering Communication*™ and the training instruments *The Neurolinguistic Communication Profile* and *Rapport: Matching and Mirroring* are available from Organization Design and Development, King of Prussia, PA, (215) 279-2002.

The book *Making The Message Clear* is available from Metamorphous Advanced Product Services, Portland, OR, 1-800-233-MAPS.

METAMORPHOUS
Advanced
Product
Services

Metamorphous Advanced Product Services (M.A.P.S.) is the master distributor for Grinder, DeLozier & Associates and other fine publishers.

M.A.P.S. offers books, cassettes, videos, software, and miscellaneous products in the following subjects; Bodywork, Business & Sales; Children; Education; Enneagram; Health; (including Alexander Technique and Rolfing); Hypnosis; Personal Development; Psychology (including Neurolinguistic Programming); and Relationships/Sexuality.

If you cannot find our books at your favorite bookstore, you can order directly from M.A.P.S.

TO ORDER OR REQUEST A FREE CATALOG:

MAIL   M.A.P.S.
P.O. Box 10616
Portland, OR 97210-0616

FAX   (503) 223-9117

CALL   Toll free 1-800-233-MAPS

CUSTOMER SERVICE AND ALL OTHER BUSINESS:

CALL   (503) 228-4972